NFS: Simplified Network File Systems

James Relington

DEDICATION

To those who seek knowledge, inspiration, and new perspectives—
may this book be a companion on your journey, a spark for curiosity,
and a reminder that every page turned is a step toward discovery.

AKNOWLEDGEMENTS

I would like to express my deepest gratitude to everyone who contributed to the creation of this book. To my colleagues and mentors, your insights and expertise have been invaluable. A special thank you to my family and friends for their unwavering support and encouragement throughout this journey.

Introduction to NFS

Network File System, commonly known as NFS, is a distributed file system protocol that allows users to access files over a network in much the same way they access local storage. Originally developed by Sun Microsystems in 1984, NFS has become a cornerstone of network storage solutions in both small-scale environments and large enterprises. The idea behind NFS was revolutionary for its time, allowing remote systems to share directories and files seamlessly across networked computers. By providing a transparent method for clients to mount remote file systems and interact with them as if they were on their local machines, NFS solved one of the fundamental challenges of early network computing: how to share data efficiently and reliably over a network.

At its core, NFS operates on a client-server model, where one or more servers export file systems, and multiple clients access these exports via network protocols. This model allows organizations to centralize their data management, providing simplified backup strategies, consistent data access policies, and efficient resource utilization. The server, which is responsible for storing and serving the data, grants access permissions to clients. These clients, in turn, request access to the files over a network, commonly using protocols such as TCP or UDP to communicate.

One of the reasons NFS gained widespread popularity is its integration with UNIX and UNIX-like operating systems. Early on, NFS was embedded within the UNIX ecosystem, making it the de facto standard for file sharing in these environments. Over time, support expanded to other operating systems, including Linux, BSD variants, and even Windows, further solidifying NFS's role as a versatile and cross-platform file-sharing solution. Its compatibility with different systems meant that organizations could create heterogeneous environments, seamlessly integrating various operating systems while maintaining a unified storage access methodology.

Technically, NFS relies on Remote Procedure Calls (RPC) to facilitate communication between client and server. RPC is a protocol that enables a program to execute code on a remote server as if it were a local function. This abstraction allowed NFS clients to interact with files over the network without needing to understand the server's underlying file system. Instead, clients issue RPC commands, and the server processes these requests, sending back the necessary data or status responses. This mechanism, though seemingly simple, laid the foundation for many modern distributed systems and influenced the development of other network file systems.

Over the years, NFS has undergone significant changes and improvements. The first version, NFSv2, was relatively simple and lacked advanced features such as file locking or strong security mechanisms. As network demands grew and environments became more complex, newer versions like NFSv3 and NFSv4 introduced critical enhancements. NFSv3 added support for larger file sizes, asynchronous writes, and more robust error handling. NFSv4, however, was a major evolution, bringing with it built-in security via Kerberos, stateful protocol design, support for Access Control Lists (ACLs), and improved performance. Each iteration addressed limitations of its predecessors, keeping NFS relevant in modern computing.

The functionality provided by NFS is particularly important in collaborative environments where multiple users or applications need to access shared data concurrently. For instance, in research institutions, development teams, and media production houses, NFS facilitates collaborative workflows by enabling users to read and write to shared directories from multiple workstations. Similarly, in enterprise data centers, NFS serves as a backbone for centralizing storage infrastructure, powering applications, databases, and user data directories.

Another critical advantage of NFS is its transparency. From the perspective of the end user, accessing a file via NFS feels no different than interacting with a file on a local hard drive. Mounting an NFS share on a client system integrates it directly into the directory hierarchy, making remote files appear as part of the local file system. This seamless integration simplifies the user experience and reduces the learning curve for end users. System administrators also benefit from this transparency, as it allows for centralized control over storage resources while maintaining flexibility for clients.

Despite its strengths, NFS is not without its challenges. Because it was designed during a time when security threats were less pervasive, early versions lacked encryption and strong authentication mechanisms. In open networks or over the internet, this posed a significant security risk. However, these concerns were addressed in later versions, particularly with the introduction of NFSv4, which included stronger security models such as RPCSEC_GSS with Kerberos authentication. Even so, many organizations choose to combine NFS with additional layers of network security, such as Virtual Private Networks (VPNs) or secure tunnels, to protect data in transit.

Today, NFS continues to evolve. It is widely used not only in traditional data centers but also in cloud environments and hybrid infrastructures. Many cloud providers offer NFS-based storage solutions as part of their services, enabling organizations to extend their on-premises infrastructure into the cloud without major architectural changes. The emergence of containerization and orchestration tools like Kubernetes has also influenced how NFS is implemented, with persistent storage volumes often relying on NFS to provide a reliable and shared storage backend for containerized applications.

Ultimately, NFS is a testament to the enduring importance of simplicity and standardization in network computing. Its design prioritizes interoperability, ease of deployment, and flexibility, characteristics that continue to make it a valuable tool in modern IT ecosystems. Whether used in a small home lab or a sprawling corporate infrastructure, NFS serves as a reliable and efficient solution for sharing data across networks. The protocol's longevity and adaptability are clear indicators of its relevance and resilience in a world where data sharing and accessibility remain paramount.

The Evolution of Network File Systems

The concept of sharing files across multiple computers has existed since the early days of networked computing. As organizations grew and computing environments became more complex, the need to efficiently and reliably share data between systems became a critical challenge. The earliest attempts at creating networked storage solutions were rudimentary, often involving manual file transfers using removable media or simple file copy commands over basic network protocols. However, as networking technology advanced, so did the demand for systems that could allow remote computers to access and manipulate files as if they were stored locally. This demand paved the way for the development of Network File Systems (NFS) and other distributed file-sharing protocols.

In the 1970s and early 1980s, as the adoption of UNIX systems spread throughout academic institutions and businesses, file sharing became increasingly important. Early solutions included protocols like the rcp (remote copy) and ftp (file transfer protocol), which allowed users to transfer files from one system to another. While these tools served their purpose, they lacked the seamlessness and transparency required for more integrated environments. Users needed a solution where remote files could be accessed without having to explicitly copy them back and forth. The need for a more native approach to file sharing drove the development of dedicated network file systems.

In 1984, Sun Microsystems introduced the Network File System, or NFS, as a way to provide UNIX clients with transparent access to remote file systems over a network. NFS was a game-changer, offering a stateless protocol based on the Remote Procedure Call (RPC) framework. This approach allowed client machines to mount directories from remote servers and interact with them as if they were part of the local file system. NFS quickly gained traction due to its simplicity, efficiency, and the fact that it was deeply integrated into UNIX-based operating systems. By the late 1980s, NFS had become the de facto standard for network file sharing in many UNIX environments.

Around the same time, other vendors and organizations were working on alternative network file systems. IBM developed the Distributed Data Management (DDM) protocol, while Digital Equipment Corporation introduced DECnet for their VMS systems. However, one of the most notable competitors to NFS was Microsoft's Server Message Block (SMB) protocol. Originally developed by IBM in the 1980s and later adopted and extended by Microsoft, SMB provided file and printer sharing capabilities for DOS and Windows-based networks. While NFS became dominant in UNIX ecosystems, SMB became the standard for Windows environments, and each evolved along its own path to meet the needs of their respective platforms.

The 1990s marked a period of further diversification and refinement in the field of network file systems. As networks became faster and storage demands grew, new protocols and distributed file systems emerged. The Andrew File System (AFS), developed at Carnegie Mellon University, introduced the concept of a location-transparent namespace and client-side caching to improve performance and scalability. AFS was adopted in large academic and research networks, and later commercialized by Transarc Corporation. Its hierarchical structure and focus on security and scalability influenced future developments in the field, including concepts that would be incorporated into modern distributed file systems.

Another significant advancement during this period was the rise of distributed file systems designed for high-performance computing and enterprise environments. The General Parallel File System (GPFS), developed by IBM, and the Parallel Virtual File System (PVFS), developed at Argonne National Laboratory, were designed to provide high-speed file access across large clusters of computers. These systems prioritized scalability and performance, addressing the unique challenges posed by supercomputing and data-intensive workloads.

As the 2000s approached, the rise of open-source software and the rapid adoption of Linux further accelerated the development of network file systems. NFS continued to evolve with the release of NFSv3, which introduced support for larger file sizes, asynchronous writes, and improved error handling. NFSv4, released in 2000, marked a major evolution, adding stateful communication, stronger security through Kerberos integration, and support for Access Control Lists (ACLs). The goal of NFSv4 was to address many of the limitations of earlier versions while remaining backward-compatible with existing UNIX and Linux systems. Its adoption was gradual but steady, especially in environments where enhanced security and performance were required.

During this same period, Microsoft continued to improve SMB, introducing SMBv2 with Windows Vista and SMBv3 with Windows 8 and Windows Server 2012. These newer versions of SMB brought significant performance enhancements, stronger encryption, and support for modern data center features like scale-out file shares and transparent failover. Meanwhile, cross-platform solutions like Samba enabled UNIX and Linux systems to communicate with SMB-based networks, bridging the gap between NFS and SMB environments and fostering greater interoperability.

The explosion of cloud computing in the 2010s brought about yet another evolution in network file systems. Organizations increasingly moved their workloads to cloud platforms, necessitating file systems that could span across on-premises data centers and public cloud infrastructure. Services like Amazon Elastic File System (EFS) and Google Cloud Filestore emerged, offering NFS-compatible storage that could be easily provisioned and scaled within cloud environments. These services provided many of the same benefits as traditional NFS but were managed and maintained by cloud providers, reducing the administrative overhead for organizations.

At the same time, object storage systems such as Amazon S3 and OpenStack Swift began gaining traction. While not traditional file systems, these object stores provided scalable, cost-effective storage for unstructured data. However, they lacked the hierarchical directory structure familiar to most users, leading to the development of gateways and adapters that translated file system protocols like NFS and SMB into object storage APIs.

In recent years, the rise of containerized applications and orchestration platforms like Kubernetes has created new challenges and opportunities for network file systems. Persistent storage for containers often relies on NFS or similar technologies to provide shared access to data across dynamic, ephemeral workloads. Modern storage solutions now focus on flexibility, scalability, and integration with automation and DevOps workflows.

The evolution of network file systems is a story of continuous innovation driven by the changing landscape of IT and the ever-growing demand for efficient data sharing. From the early days of rudimentary file transfer tools to the sophisticated distributed file systems that power today's global networks, each advancement has built upon the lessons of the past while addressing the needs of the present. As technology continues to advance, network file systems will undoubtedly remain a vital part of modern infrastructure, adapting to new paradigms such as edge computing, hybrid cloud, and AI-driven analytics.

How NFS Works: The Basics

The Network File System, or NFS, is designed to enable a client computer to access files and directories located on a remote server as if they were part of the client's own local file system. This concept, often referred to as transparent file sharing, lies at the heart of NFS's architecture and functionality. NFS operates on a client-server model where one system, acting as the server, makes directories available to other systems, known as clients. These clients then mount the shared directories, seamlessly integrating them into their local directory structure.

At its most fundamental level, NFS works by transmitting file access requests from the client to the server over a network. The client does not physically copy files from the server to its local storage. Instead, it accesses and manipulates files directly on the remote server using standard file system calls, such as read, write, open, and close. This ability allows users and applications to work with remote files in the same way they interact with local files, without requiring additional steps or specialized commands.

The client-side component of NFS starts with the mount operation. When a user or system administrator mounts an NFS export—a directory that the server has made available—the remote directory is mapped to a mount point within the client's directory hierarchy. This mount point could be any directory, such as /mnt/shared or /data/projects, depending on the administrator's preference. Once mounted, the contents of the remote directory appear as part of the local file system, and users can navigate to it using standard file browsing tools or command-line utilities.

NFS communication relies on Remote Procedure Call, or RPC, which provides the mechanism by which the client sends requests to the server and the server responds with data or status updates. RPC works by enabling the client to invoke procedures on the server system as if they were local function calls. Under the hood, these RPC calls are transmitted over the network, typically using either the Transmission Control Protocol (TCP) or the User Datagram Protocol (UDP), depending on the NFS version and configuration.

The server's role in this process is to handle incoming RPC requests and execute the requested file operations on the server's local file system. The server software listens on specific ports for incoming RPC calls and processes them by interacting with its local file system. If a client requests to open a file, the server checks file permissions, retrieves the file from disk, and sends back the necessary file metadata or data blocks. These interactions occur repeatedly during normal file operations such as reading, writing, or listing directory contents.

A key concept in NFS is that it is traditionally a stateless protocol, at least in its earlier versions. In a stateless model, the server does not keep track of client session information between requests. Each client request is treated as an independent transaction, containing all necessary information for the server to fulfill it. This statelessness simplifies server design and allows for easier recovery in the event of client or server crashes, as no persistent session data is lost. However, it also introduces limitations, such as the need for the client to reissue requests when disruptions occur.

Later versions of NFS, such as NFSv4, introduced stateful features, improving performance and functionality. NFSv4 maintains certain session-related information, such as file locks and delegations, which enhances efficiency and enables advanced capabilities like file locking and leasing. These additions help avoid conflicts when multiple clients access the same files and allow for better handling of concurrent operations.

Another essential element in the operation of NFS is the export process. On the server side, administrators specify which directories they wish to share with clients by configuring the /etc/exports file, which defines export rules and access permissions. This configuration file allows administrators to control which clients or networks have access to specific directories and whether the access is read-only or read-write. The server then makes these exports available using NFS daemons, such as nfsd, rpc.mountd, and rpc.statd, each responsible for specific tasks within the NFS workflow.

When a client mounts a remote directory, the server validates the client's credentials and applies any access control restrictions defined in the export settings. In addition to export rules, NFS also relies on file-level permissions defined by the underlying file system on the server. This means that even if a client is granted access to an exported directory, it must still adhere to the file system's standard permissions, such as read, write, and execute bits, as well as ownership constraints.

Caching plays a vital role in NFS performance. To reduce the amount of network traffic and minimize latency, NFS clients implement local caching of file data and metadata. When a client reads a file from the server, it stores portions of the file in its local memory or disk cache. Subsequent read operations can then be served from the cache, reducing the need to query the server repeatedly. However, caching introduces challenges related to data consistency, particularly in environments where multiple clients are accessing and modifying the same files. NFS addresses these challenges with mechanisms such as attribute caching timeouts and cache invalidation policies, ensuring that clients periodically verify the freshness of cached data with the server.

NFS supports both synchronous and asynchronous write operations. In synchronous mode, each write request is acknowledged by the server only after the data is committed to stable storage. This approach provides stronger data integrity but can reduce performance due to the additional latency introduced by disk writes. In asynchronous mode, the server may acknowledge write requests before the data is physically written to disk, improving performance but potentially risking data loss in the event of a server crash.

The NFS client's behavior is configurable through various mount options, such as hard or soft mounts, timeouts, retransmission counts, and read-write settings. A hard mount ensures that the client will continue retrying requests indefinitely until the server responds, which is critical for applications that require guaranteed access to data. In contrast, a soft mount allows requests to fail after a defined number of retries, reducing the chance of system hangs but potentially leading to application errors.

Overall, NFS provides a highly effective solution for sharing files across networked systems. Its design allows remote storage to be integrated seamlessly into local directory structures, while its reliance on standard file system calls ensures broad compatibility with existing applications and workflows. The basic operation of NFS revolves around this ability to abstract remote files as local resources, creating a unified and transparent environment where users and systems can collaborate and share data across diverse networked infrastructures.

NFS Architecture Overview

The architecture of the Network File System (NFS) is rooted in simplicity and modularity, which has allowed it to remain a vital component of networked storage for decades. At a high level, NFS follows a client-server model where one or more servers provide shared access to their file systems and multiple clients mount these shared file systems over a network. However, beneath this seemingly straightforward model lies a layered architecture that coordinates numerous components and protocols to provide seamless, transparent file access across distributed environments.

At its core, the NFS server is responsible for exporting directories to client systems. The export process is controlled by the server administrator, who configures which directories to share and defines access permissions for each client or network subnet. This is typically managed through the server's export table, which specifies the exported directories and associated options such as read-only or read-write access, root squash rules, and user mapping settings. The server maintains these exports and ensures that only authorized clients can mount and interact with the shared directories.

When a client system mounts a remote directory from the NFS server, it integrates the shared directory into its local file system hierarchy, making the remote files appear as if they reside locally. This mounting process is facilitated by several critical components within the NFS architecture. The first key element is the mount protocol, which is handled by the rpc.mountd daemon on the server. When a client requests to mount a directory, the mount daemon verifies the client's access permissions and returns a file handle representing the root of the exported directory.

Once the mount operation is successful, communication between the client and server is primarily handled by the NFS protocol, which operates over Remote Procedure Calls (RPC). The NFS server runs the nfsd daemon, which listens for incoming NFS requests and processes file operations such as reading, writing, opening, closing, and retrieving metadata. The stateless nature of early versions of NFS meant that each request was independent, containing all necessary information for the server to process the operation. Later versions of NFS, such as NFSv4, introduced stateful elements to improve efficiency and enable features like file locking and delegations.

The transport layer plays an important role in the NFS architecture. NFS traffic typically runs over either the User Datagram Protocol (UDP) or the Transmission Control Protocol (TCP). Early implementations of NFS primarily relied on UDP due to its low overhead and faster transmission in local area networks (LANs). However, UDP's lack of reliability mechanisms made it less suitable for wide area networks (WANs) or networks with higher latency. As a result, later versions of NFS favored TCP, which provides reliable data transmission, congestion control, and better error handling.

Beyond the nfsd and rpc.mountd daemons, additional supporting services are critical to the operation of NFS. The rpcbind service (formerly known as portmap) is responsible for mapping RPC program numbers to network ports. Because RPC programs can use dynamically assigned ports, clients must contact rpcbind on the server to determine which ports the various NFS services are using. Without rpcbind, clients would be unable to locate the correct services required for NFS communication.

Another crucial component in the NFS architecture is the Network Lock Manager (NLM), implemented through the rpc.statd and rpc.lockd daemons. In stateless versions of NFS, such as NFSv3, file locking is handled externally using NLM. When a client locks a file to prevent concurrent modifications by other clients, the lock manager ensures that the lock state is maintained and communicated between clients and the server. NFSv4, however, integrated file locking directly into the protocol itself, eliminating the need for external lock daemons.

On the client side, the NFS architecture includes a client-side NFS module, typically implemented as a kernel driver in most operating systems. This module intercepts file system calls from user applications and translates them into NFS RPC requests sent to the server. For example, when an application on the client system performs a read operation, the NFS client module packages this request into an RPC call and transmits it to the server, where it is processed by nfsd. The server then responds with the requested data, which the client module returns to the application. From the perspective of the application, this process is entirely transparent, appearing as if the data resides on a local disk.

Caching is another architectural component that impacts NFS performance and behavior. The client-side NFS module maintains local caches of file data and metadata to minimize network traffic and reduce latency. This caching mechanism stores frequently accessed data in memory, reducing the number of RPC requests sent to the server. However, caching introduces complexities related to consistency and coherency, particularly in multi-client environments where different systems may be reading from and writing to the same files. To address this, NFS employs cache invalidation strategies and attribute caching timers to periodically synchronize client caches with the server's file system state.

Security within the NFS architecture is handled at multiple layers. At the export level, the server enforces access control rules based on client IP addresses or hostnames. Additionally, NFS supports authentication mechanisms such as AUTH_SYS, which relies on client-side user and group IDs to enforce file permissions. In environments requiring stronger security, NFSv4 supports Kerberos-based authentication via the RPCSEC_GSS framework, providing integrity and privacy services for NFS operations. This enhancement is particularly valuable in enterprise environments where secure and auditable file sharing is critical.

Another architectural evolution introduced by NFSv4 is the consolidation of NFS functionality into a single, firewall-friendly port. Earlier versions of NFS required multiple daemons and ports, complicating firewall configurations. NFSv4 streamlined this by utilizing a single TCP port (2049) for all NFS operations, simplifying deployment in secure and restricted network environments.

High availability and redundancy can be built into NFS architecture through the use of clustered NFS servers and shared storage systems. By deploying multiple NFS servers connected to a shared backend storage, organizations can create failover configurations where a secondary server takes over if the primary server fails. Additionally, technologies like distributed file systems and load balancers can be integrated with NFS to improve scalability and resilience.

In contemporary IT environments, NFS is also used in conjunction with modern technologies such as virtualization platforms, container orchestration systems, and cloud-based services. NFS can serve as a shared storage solution for virtual machines, providing centralized storage for VM images and data. It can also be used to provide persistent storage for containerized applications running in Kubernetes clusters, where NFS shares are mounted as persistent volumes accessible across multiple pods.

The modular and layered architecture of NFS is what allows it to function efficiently across such diverse environments. By separating responsibilities between daemons, leveraging standard protocols like RPC, and providing both stateless and stateful operation modes, NFS achieves the flexibility and reliability required for modern distributed systems. From its early use in simple LAN setups to its integration in complex hybrid cloud infrastructures, the NFS architecture continues to evolve, adapting to the changing landscape of enterprise and cloud computing.

RPC and XDR in NFS Communication

At the heart of NFS communication lies a set of essential technologies that make remote file access possible. Among these, Remote Procedure Call (RPC) and External Data Representation (XDR) play crucial roles in how clients and servers exchange information. Understanding these technologies is key to grasping how NFS operates behind the scenes. Both RPC and XDR are foundational building blocks that allow NFS to function as a distributed file system, enabling seamless data exchange across heterogeneous systems and networks.

Remote Procedure Call, or RPC, is a communication paradigm that enables a program to execute procedures on another machine as if they were local function calls. This abstraction simplifies the development of distributed applications, as the details of network communication are handled transparently by the RPC mechanism. In the context of NFS, RPC provides the mechanism through which client systems request file operations from remote servers. These operations include opening files, reading data, writing data, closing files, and querying file attributes. The client does not need to know how these tasks are performed internally on the server; it simply invokes RPC calls that are executed remotely.

RPC operates using a client-server model. The NFS client, when issuing a file system request, generates an RPC call that is transmitted over the network to the NFS server. The server, upon receiving this call, executes the corresponding file operation and returns a response. This back-and-forth communication is the core of NFS's distributed nature, and RPC ensures that it happens reliably and efficiently. RPC is designed to be transport-independent, meaning it can function over different network protocols such as UDP or TCP, depending on the environment and configuration.

One of the strengths of RPC is its ability to handle procedure calls as if they were part of the local execution flow. For instance, when an application on the client system attempts to read a file from an NFS mount, the NFS client module issues an RPC read request to the server. The server processes this request by accessing its local file system and reading the requested data. It then sends the data back to the client in an RPC response. To the application, this process is indistinguishable from reading a local file, even though network communication and remote procedure execution are occurring in the background.

RPC is also crucial for managing various NFS-related services beyond basic file operations. For example, services such as rpc.mountd and rpc.lockd also rely on RPC to handle mount requests and file locking mechanisms, respectively. These services are defined as individual RPC programs with unique program numbers and sets of procedures that clients can invoke. To locate these services, clients use the rpcbind service, which maintains a registry of RPC programs and the ports on which they are listening. Once a client learns the correct port number from rpcbind, it can send RPC requests directly to the appropriate service.

While RPC facilitates remote procedure execution, there is also a need to ensure that the data transmitted between client and server is represented in a consistent format, regardless of the underlying hardware or operating system. This is where External Data Representation, or XDR, comes into play. XDR is a standard for the platform-independent representation of data structures. It ensures that data encoded by one machine can be correctly interpreted by another, even if the two systems have different architectures, such as varying endianness or data type sizes.

NFS, like other RPC-based systems, relies on XDR to serialize and deserialize data exchanged between clients and servers. When the client issues an RPC call, the data payload is encoded using XDR, transforming native data structures into a standardized binary format. The server then decodes this payload, processes the request, and encodes the response using XDR before sending it back to the client.

Upon receipt, the client decodes the response and returns the data to the application.

This serialization process is essential for achieving interoperability between diverse systems. In an environment where NFS clients and servers might run different operating systems or be built on different processor architectures, XDR guarantees that both sides can understand and correctly process the data they exchange. This capability is especially important in enterprise environments where NFS is often deployed across heterogeneous networks that include Linux, UNIX, BSD, and even Windows systems via tools like Samba.

XDR is designed to be simple and efficient, supporting common data types such as integers, floating-point numbers, fixed-length arrays, variable-length arrays, and more complex structures such as unions and records. It defines how each data type should be represented in the binary stream, including how to handle padding and alignment. This consistency ensures that when data is encoded on the client, it arrives on the server in a format that the server's RPC library can reliably decode.

Another important aspect of RPC and XDR in NFS communication is their extensibility. As new versions of NFS were developed, such as NFSv3 and NFSv4, new procedures and data structures were added to the protocol. Thanks to the modular nature of RPC and the flexibility of XDR, these updates could be incorporated without requiring a complete redesign of the underlying communication framework. Instead, new RPC program numbers and procedure identifiers were introduced, and new data types were defined within the existing XDR specifications.

Error handling is another area where RPC plays a vital role. If a server fails to respond to a client's RPC request due to a network disruption or service failure, the RPC framework on the client side automatically retries the request according to predefined timeout and retransmission settings. This behavior contributes to NFS's resilience, allowing it to recover gracefully from transient network issues or server reboots. On the server side, if a malformed or incomplete RPC request is received, the server's RPC implementation can reject the request and return an appropriate error message to the client.

As NFS evolved, so did the use of RPC and XDR. In NFSv4, for example, a stateful protocol design was introduced along with additional RPC procedures for managing client sessions, delegations, and more sophisticated file locking mechanisms. Despite these advancements, the fundamental reliance on RPC for communication and XDR for data representation remained intact. These technologies continue to underpin the reliable and platform-agnostic communication model that NFS depends on.

Ultimately, RPC and XDR work together to create a robust and interoperable foundation for NFS communication. RPC abstracts the complexity of remote procedure execution, while XDR ensures consistent data formatting across disparate systems. This combination allows NFS to provide a seamless file-sharing experience in environments ranging from small office networks to large-scale enterprise data centers, maintaining reliable and efficient communication between clients and servers across diverse network topologies.

NFS vs. Other Network File Systems

Network file systems are critical components of modern computing environments, providing shared access to data across multiple machines over a network. While the Network File System (NFS) is one of the most widely adopted solutions, it is far from the only option available. Other network file systems, such as Server Message Block (SMB), Andrew File System (AFS), CephFS, and GlusterFS, each bring their own features, design philosophies, and use cases to the table. Comparing NFS to these alternatives helps to better understand its unique position, strengths, and limitations within the landscape of distributed file systems.

NFS was originally designed for UNIX systems and has evolved into a broadly supported, open standard that facilitates seamless file sharing across UNIX, Linux, BSD, and other UNIX-like environments. It is known for its simplicity and tight integration with native file system operations. NFS allows clients to mount remote directories directly into their local file system hierarchy, giving users and applications a transparent experience as if they were interacting with a local disk. This level of integration is one of the key advantages of NFS, making it easy to deploy and manage in UNIX-centric environments.

In contrast, SMB, originally developed by IBM and later heavily extended by Microsoft, is the dominant file-sharing protocol in Windows environments. While NFS and SMB serve similar purposes, there are notable differences in design and implementation. SMB is a stateful protocol, maintaining session information between client and server, while earlier versions of NFS were stateless, treating each client request as an independent transaction. The stateful nature of SMB enables features such as session recovery and opportunistic locking, which optimize performance in Windows networks by reducing redundant data transfer and improving file consistency across clients.

SMB also offers rich integration with Windows-specific technologies such as Active Directory for centralized authentication, Group Policy enforcement, and native support for Windows file and share permissions. This tight integration makes SMB the natural choice for Windows-based networks and organizations that rely on Microsoft ecosystems. However, SMB has historically been viewed as more complex to configure and less performant in certain scenarios, particularly in mixed-OS environments where compatibility issues may arise. Samba, an open-source implementation of SMB, bridges this gap by enabling UNIX and Linux systems to act as both SMB clients and servers, providing cross-platform file sharing between UNIX and Windows hosts.

AFS, developed at Carnegie Mellon University and later commercialized by Transarc Corporation, introduces a fundamentally different approach to distributed file systems. AFS emphasizes a global namespace, location transparency, and client-side caching. Unlike NFS and SMB, AFS was designed with scalability and security as top priorities, particularly for large, distributed organizations. Its global namespace allows users to access files without knowing their physical location on the network, simplifying data management in environments with geographically dispersed users and servers. Additionally, AFS includes built-in Kerberos-based authentication, strong access control mechanisms, and an efficient caching system that reduces the load on servers by allowing clients to cache entire files locally.

While AFS excels in academic and research environments where large numbers of users need to access shared data across multiple sites, it is less commonly used in modern enterprise IT compared to NFS or SMB. This is due in part to its complex setup, maintenance requirements, and the limited ecosystem support compared to more widely adopted protocols.

Another major player in the network file system arena is CephFS, a component of the Ceph distributed storage system. CephFS is a highly scalable, POSIX-compliant file system designed for distributed environments. Unlike NFS, which traditionally relies on a central server to manage file access, CephFS is built on a decentralized architecture where data is distributed across multiple storage nodes using a Reliable Autonomic Distributed Object Store (RADOS) layer. This design eliminates single points of failure and allows CephFS to scale horizontally, handling petabytes of data and thousands of clients efficiently.

CephFS also includes advanced features such as dynamic striping, snapshots, and metadata clustering, which are well-suited for environments where performance and redundancy are critical. CephFS is often favored in modern cloud-native and high-performance computing environments due to its ability to provide block, object, and file storage from a single platform. However, its deployment and management can be significantly more complex than traditional NFS setups, often requiring specialized knowledge and robust orchestration tools to ensure optimal performance and fault tolerance.

Similarly, GlusterFS is another distributed file system that has gained popularity for its ability to aggregate storage resources from multiple servers into a single global namespace. GlusterFS, like CephFS, is designed for scalability and high availability, using a modular, stackable architecture that allows administrators to customize storage configurations based on specific workload requirements. It provides features such as replication, striping, and geo-replication, making it suitable for large-scale deployments where data redundancy and disaster recovery are important.

Unlike NFS, which generally relies on a dedicated server-client model, GlusterFS allows all nodes in the cluster to act as both servers and clients. This peer-to-peer architecture facilitates load balancing and reduces the risk of bottlenecks associated with centralized servers. While GlusterFS offers flexibility and resilience, it also introduces additional complexity in terms of deployment, monitoring, and troubleshooting, making it more suitable for organizations with experienced storage teams.

When comparing NFS to these alternatives, one of its most defining characteristics is its simplicity and ubiquity. NFS is supported out-of-the-box on nearly every UNIX and Linux distribution, making it an ideal choice for environments that require quick, straightforward file sharing without extensive configuration or infrastructure overhead. Additionally, NFS's integration with native UNIX permission models and its mature ecosystem of tools contribute to its reliability and ease of use.

However, NFS also has limitations. In its traditional form, NFS relies heavily on underlying network stability and does not provide built-in redundancy or high-availability features. While techniques such as deploying NFS on top of clustered file systems or using network failover mechanisms can mitigate these issues, protocols like CephFS and GlusterFS are inherently designed to handle node failures and dynamic scaling. Furthermore, while NFSv4 introduced stateful capabilities and enhanced security features, older versions of NFS lack the built-in encryption and robust authentication mechanisms found in protocols like SMB and AFS.

Each network file system has strengths tailored to specific use cases. NFS is highly effective for UNIX-based environments where ease of deployment, low overhead, and native system integration are prioritized. SMB excels in Windows-centric environments requiring advanced Windows-native features. AFS is suited for distributed, multi-site organizations seeking a global namespace and strong security, while CephFS and GlusterFS address the demands of highly scalable, resilient storage infrastructures in modern cloud and enterprise deployments.

Ultimately, the choice between NFS and other network file systems depends on factors such as the organization's existing infrastructure, scalability needs, security requirements, and administrative expertise. While NFS continues to be a trusted solution for many, other file systems may offer compelling advantages in specific scenarios where distributed architecture, advanced redundancy, or integrated object and block storage are essential.

NFS Protocol Versions: From v2 to v4.2

The Network File System has evolved significantly since its introduction, with each new protocol version addressing limitations of previous iterations and introducing new features to meet the demands of increasingly complex computing environments. The journey of NFS from version 2 to version 4.2 illustrates the progressive refinement of distributed file system technology and its adaptation to modern IT infrastructures.

NFS version 2, introduced by Sun Microsystems in 1984, laid the groundwork for remote file sharing over networks. NFSv2 was designed as a stateless protocol running over the Remote Procedure Call (RPC) system. It allowed UNIX clients to mount file systems exported by remote servers and access them as though they were local. This early version operated exclusively over the User Datagram Protocol (UDP), providing low overhead and fast performance in local area networks. However, it was limited by its reliance on 32-bit file offsets, restricting it to handling files no larger than 2 gigabytes. NFSv2 also lacked support for more advanced features like file locking, symbolic links management, and finer-grained security controls.

As the demand for more robust and scalable file-sharing solutions grew, NFS version 3 emerged in 1995 to address many of the shortcomings of its predecessor. NFSv3 introduced support for 64-bit file offsets, enabling the handling of files larger than 2 gigabytes, which was increasingly necessary as file sizes ballooned with the rise of multimedia content and large-scale scientific datasets. NFSv3 also added asynchronous writes, which allowed the server to acknowledge write requests before the data was written to disk, significantly improving performance in many workloads.

Another key enhancement in NFSv3 was the introduction of improved error reporting, offering more precise feedback to clients when operations failed. This version also expanded the set of supported file attributes, such as creation time, and introduced READDIRPLUS, a procedure that allowed clients to retrieve file attributes along with directory listings in a single request, reducing the number of round trips required between client and server. NFSv3 could operate over both UDP and TCP, with TCP offering greater reliability for wide-area networks and environments where packet loss or network instability could impact performance.

Despite the improvements in NFSv3, challenges related to security, state management, and cross-platform compatibility persisted. To address these, NFS version 4 was introduced in 2000 as a major redesign of the protocol. Unlike its stateless predecessors, NFSv4 adopted a stateful approach to client-server communication, maintaining session information to enable advanced features like file locking and delegations. Delegations allow the server to grant temporary exclusive rights to a client for file operations, reducing the need for frequent server interaction and improving performance in certain workloads.

NFSv4 consolidated many of the auxiliary protocols used by earlier versions into a single protocol. For example, mounting file systems and performing locking operations were previously handled by separate services, such as rpc.mountd and the Network Lock Manager (NLM). NFSv4 integrated these functionalities directly into the core protocol, simplifying firewall configuration and reducing the number of services needed for full operation. Additionally, NFSv4 mandated the use of TCP as its transport protocol, benefiting from its reliability and congestion control mechanisms.

Security was a major focus of NFSv4. It introduced support for RPCSEC_GSS, which enabled stronger authentication mechanisms such as Kerberos, as well as optional data integrity and privacy through cryptographic methods. NFSv4 also brought support for Access Control Lists (ACLs), providing more granular permissions compared to the traditional UNIX file permission model. These features made NFSv4 more suitable for enterprise environments where compliance and security were critical concerns.

Building on the advancements of NFSv4, NFS version 4.1, standardized in 2010, further enhanced the protocol's capabilities, particularly for high-performance and large-scale environments. One of the most significant innovations in NFSv4.1 was the introduction of the Parallel NFS (pNFS) extension. pNFS aimed to address performance bottlenecks by decoupling metadata and data access. In a traditional NFS setup, clients communicate with a single server for both metadata and data operations. With pNFS, clients can retrieve metadata from a metadata server and access the actual data directly from multiple storage servers in parallel, improving throughput and scalability.

NFSv4.1 also introduced sessions, a mechanism that improved the handling of failures and enhanced client-server communication efficiency. Sessions allow for the tracking of outstanding requests, enabling features like replay protection, where duplicate requests caused by network failures can be safely ignored by the server. This greatly improved the robustness of NFS in distributed environments, especially those with unreliable networks or failover configurations.

Following NFSv4.1, NFS version 4.2, finalized in 2016, expanded the protocol further with a focus on improving flexibility and storage efficiency. NFSv4.2 added several important features, including server-side copy (SSC), which allows the server to perform file copies internally without transferring data over the network. This significantly reduces network load and speeds up copy operations, particularly for large files.

Another notable addition in NFSv4.2 is the sparse file and space reservation support. Sparse files are files that contain large blocks of zeros which do not physically consume disk space. With this feature, NFS clients can create sparse files and reserve space on the server's storage, optimizing storage utilization. NFSv4.2 also introduced application I/O hints, enabling clients to provide the server with information about their intended I/O patterns. These hints can help the server optimize storage layouts or caching strategies based on the workload.

Extended attribute (xattr) support in NFSv4.2 provided clients with the ability to associate arbitrary metadata with files, such as security labels or application-specific data. This feature is especially useful in security-conscious environments or those utilizing mandatory access control systems like SELinux. Additionally, NFSv4.2 introduced SEEK operations, enabling efficient detection of data and hole regions in sparse files, further improving I/O performance for certain applications.

Throughout the evolution from NFSv2 to NFSv4.2, backward compatibility has remained a guiding principle. While newer versions introduced significant enhancements, they retained the core semantics and behaviors of earlier versions, ensuring that existing applications and workflows could continue to function with minimal modification. This commitment to compatibility has contributed to NFS's longevity and widespread adoption across diverse computing environments.

Each step in the progression of NFS versions reflects an ongoing effort to balance simplicity, performance, security, and scalability. While NFSv2 and NFSv3 provided lightweight, stateless solutions ideal for simpler networked environments, the shift to statefulness and integrated security in NFSv4 addressed the growing complexity and demands of modern enterprise and cloud-based infrastructures. The addition of pNFS and further optimizations in NFSv4.1 and NFSv4.2 positioned NFS as a viable solution even for high-performance computing and large-scale storage environments where throughput, flexibility, and data integrity are critical.

The evolution of NFS protocol versions showcases the dynamic nature of distributed storage technology and how it continuously adapts to new challenges and opportunities in networking, security, and data management.

NFS Components and Daemons

The Network File System is composed of several critical components and background processes, commonly referred to as daemons, that work together to enable the seamless sharing and accessing of remote file systems across a network. These components are essential to the functioning of both the server and client sides of NFS. Each plays a specialized role in handling specific aspects of communication, authentication, resource management, and file system operations. Understanding how these components interact is crucial to effectively deploying, managing, and troubleshooting NFS in any environment.

At the core of the NFS server is the nfsd daemon, which is responsible for handling file system requests from NFS clients. This daemon processes client RPC (Remote Procedure Call) requests and performs corresponding operations on the server's local file system, such as reading, writing, or modifying files. The nfsd daemon is the heart of the NFS service, as it translates network-based file operations into local file system actions. The server can run multiple instances of nfsd to handle concurrent requests and distribute the workload across multiple CPU cores, improving scalability and responsiveness under heavy loads.

Supporting nfsd is the rpc.mountd daemon, which plays a critical role during the initial mount operation when clients request to mount an exported directory from the server. The rpc.mountd daemon validates whether the requesting client has permission to access the export by referencing the server's export configuration, usually located in the /etc/exports file. It checks client IP addresses, access control lists, and export options such as read-only or read-write permissions. Once validation is successful, rpc.mountd provides the client with a file handle that represents the root of the exported directory, enabling the client to begin interacting with the remote file system.

The rpcbind service, sometimes referred to by its older name, portmap, is another fundamental component in the NFS architecture. RPC-based services, including NFS and its associated daemons, use dynamically assigned ports for communication. The rpcbind service maintains a registry that maps RPC program numbers to their respective port numbers. When an NFS client initiates communication, it first contacts rpcbind on the server to discover which ports the nfsd, rpc.mountd, and other daemons are using. Without rpcbind, clients would be unable to locate the appropriate ports to establish a connection, effectively blocking NFS operations.

Locking is an essential feature for maintaining data consistency when multiple clients access shared files simultaneously. To manage file locking in NFS versions prior to NFSv4, the rpc.statd and rpc.lockd daemons are employed. The rpc.lockd daemon is responsible for processing client file lock and unlock requests. When a client locks a file, rpc.lockd ensures that no other client can modify the file until the lock is released. This mechanism is vital in environments where concurrent access to shared files is common. The rpc.statd daemon works in tandem with rpc.lockd by handling crash recovery and monitoring the state of client systems. If a client holding a lock crashes or becomes unreachable, rpc.statd helps resolve stale locks and notifies the server so it can reclaim resources and prevent deadlocks.

With the introduction of NFSv4, many of these functions were integrated directly into the protocol itself. NFSv4 eliminated the need for external locking daemons by embedding file locking and state management into its core design. However, older versions of NFS, such as NFSv3, still depend on rpc.statd and rpc.lockd for proper lock handling. Even with NFSv4, rpcbind may still be required for backward compatibility in environments running mixed protocol versions or legacy systems.

The exportfs utility is another key component in the NFS ecosystem. It is used by administrators to maintain and refresh the list of exported directories on the server. While editing the /etc/exports file defines which directories are shared, running exportfs allows the server to apply these changes in real-time. Exportfs can display active exports, remove exports from the server's export table, or re-export directories without requiring a full restart of the NFS service. This utility is essential for dynamic environments where export configurations may change frequently.

On the client side, the NFS architecture relies on the NFS client module, typically implemented as part of the operating system's kernel. This module is responsible for intercepting file system calls made by applications and translating them into NFS RPC requests directed at the remote server. The client module handles mounting remote file systems, managing caches, and interacting with other system services to ensure a smooth integration of remote directories into the client's local file hierarchy. Most UNIX-like operating systems, including Linux, FreeBSD, and Solaris, include native support for the NFS client module.

Client systems also make use of mount utilities, such as the mount command, to connect to NFS shares. By specifying the NFS server's hostname or IP address and the path of the exported directory, clients can mount remote file systems into their local directory tree. Various mount options are available to configure behavior such as read-write access, timeouts, caching policies, and transport protocol preferences. Once mounted, the remote directory is accessible like any other local directory, enabling applications to read and write files without modification.

Caching is an integral part of NFS performance optimization, and the client module implements several caching layers to reduce network traffic and latency. These include attribute caching, where file metadata such as permissions and timestamps are stored temporarily, and data caching, where file contents are cached locally. While caching improves performance, it also introduces potential consistency challenges, as multiple clients might cache outdated data. To mitigate this, NFS implements mechanisms for cache validation and timeout settings that control how frequently clients check with the server for updates.

Another client-side component is the automounter, commonly implemented as the autofs service in Linux environments. The automounter dynamically mounts NFS shares on-demand when a directory is accessed and automatically unmounts them after a period of inactivity. This reduces the need for static mount entries in system configuration files and helps optimize resource usage by ensuring that NFS mounts are only active when needed.

For secure NFS deployments, additional components such as Kerberos and the rpc.gssd and rpc.svcgssd daemons come into play. These daemons facilitate the use of Kerberos authentication with NFSv4, providing strong security features such as mutual authentication, integrity checking, and data encryption. The rpc.gssd daemon runs on the client side, handling authentication tickets and security contexts, while rpc.svcgssd operates on the server, verifying client credentials and managing secure sessions.

Collectively, these components and daemons form the backbone of NFS's operation. They coordinate to provide a reliable and efficient file-sharing service across diverse network environments. From validating client access and mounting directories to processing file operations and managing locking, each element contributes to NFS's ability to offer transparent, scalable, and secure file sharing in distributed systems. Their interplay allows administrators to tailor NFS implementations to suit a variety of use cases, from small office networks to large-scale enterprise deployments with demanding performance and security requirements.

Setting Up an NFS Server

Deploying an NFS server is a fundamental task in enabling file sharing across multiple systems in a network. The process involves several key steps, from installing the necessary software packages to configuring exports and tuning security and performance settings. Setting up an NFS server provides centralized storage that multiple clients can access as if it were part of their local file system. This capability is essential in environments ranging from small workgroups to large enterprise networks.

The first step in setting up an NFS server is to ensure that the system designated as the server has all the required NFS packages installed. Most modern Linux distributions, such as Ubuntu, CentOS, or Debian, include NFS server software within their default package repositories. The main package is typically called nfs-utils or nfs-kernel-server, depending on the distribution. Installing these packages provides the server with the core NFS daemons, such as nfsd and rpc.mountd, which are essential for handling client requests and managing exports.

Once the software is installed, the next task is to configure the directories that will be shared with clients. This is done by editing the /etc/exports file, which serves as the configuration file for NFS exports. Each line in this file defines a directory to be shared and the access rules associated with it. For example, a common configuration might specify that a directory such as /srv/nfs/projects is to be shared with all clients in a specific subnet, with options that define whether clients have read-only or read-write access. Administrators can also specify additional parameters, such as sync or async behavior, and control how root users from client machines are mapped on the server.

An example export entry might look like this: /srv/nfs/projects 192.168.1.0/24(rw,sync,no_root_squash), where /srv/nfs/projects is the directory to be shared, and the access control is limited to the 192.168.1.0/24 subnet. The rw option grants read and write access, while sync ensures that write operations are committed to the disk before the server responds to the client, promoting data integrity. The no_root_squash option prevents the root user on the client from being mapped to the anonymous user on the server, which is useful in certain controlled environments but can introduce security risks if used indiscriminately.

After editing the /etc/exports file, the exportfs utility is used to apply the changes. Running exportfs -ra re-reads the configuration file and updates the list of active exports without requiring a full restart of the NFS service. Administrators can verify which directories are currently being shared by running exportfs -v, which displays all active exports along with their configured options.

The NFS server daemons must then be started and enabled to run at system boot. This typically involves starting the nfs-server, rpcbind, and nfs-mountd services. Most distributions use systemd as the service manager, so the relevant commands would be systemctl start nfs-server and systemctl enable nfs-server to ensure the service is both started and persistent across reboots. The rpcbind service should also be started, as it is necessary for clients to locate the correct NFS services and ports on the server.

Firewall configuration is another critical aspect of setting up an NFS server. By default, NFS operates over several ports, including TCP/UDP port 2049 for the nfsd daemon and additional ports for auxiliary services such as rpc.mountd and rpc.statd. Depending on the distribution, these ports may be dynamic unless explicitly configured. To simplify firewall rules and ensure secure operation, administrators often choose to assign static ports to these services by modifying the relevant configuration files. Once the ports are determined, firewall rules can be created to allow traffic from trusted networks while blocking unwanted access.

For example, using firewalld on a Red Hat-based system, an administrator might execute firewall-cmd --add-service=nfs --permanent and firewall-cmd --reload to allow NFS traffic through the firewall. Alternatively, specific ports can be opened individually for finer-grained control. Limiting access to specific IP ranges or subnets further enhances security by ensuring that only authorized clients can connect to the NFS server.

Security is paramount in NFS deployments, especially when data is shared across untrusted or public networks. By default, NFS relies on client-side user and group IDs to enforce file permissions, which can be a vulnerability if not properly managed. To address this, administrators should ensure that user and group IDs are consistent across client and server systems or implement NFSv4 with Kerberos authentication, which provides stronger security through mutual authentication and encrypted sessions.

Kerberos integration requires additional setup, including configuring the server and clients to join the same Kerberos realm, creating service principals, and deploying rpc.gssd and rpc.svcgssd daemons for handling secure authentication. When configured correctly, NFSv4 with Kerberos significantly reduces the risk of unauthorized access or credential spoofing.

Performance tuning is another consideration when setting up an NFS server. Factors such as read and write block sizes (rsize and wsize), the number of nfsd threads, and caching policies can impact the efficiency of file operations. These parameters can be adjusted to suit the specific workload characteristics of the environment. For example, increasing the number of nfsd threads allows the server to handle more simultaneous client requests, which is essential in high-traffic environments.

In addition to performance tuning, administrators may also configure the NFS server to work in high-availability or clustered environments. By combining NFS with shared storage solutions and clustering technologies such as Pacemaker and Corosync, it is possible to build redundant NFS servers that provide failover capabilities, ensuring continuous availability even if one node fails.

Once the server is fully configured, clients can mount the exported directories using the mount command, specifying the server's hostname or IP address along with the export path. For example, mount -t nfs server:/srv/nfs/projects /mnt/projects would mount the shared directory to the local /mnt/projects directory. Clients can also add persistent entries to their /etc/fstab file to ensure that NFS shares are automatically mounted at boot.

Proper monitoring and logging are essential to maintaining an NFS server. Logs related to NFS activity are typically stored in system log files, such as /var/log/messages or /var/log/syslog, depending on the system. Monitoring tools like nfsstat provide valuable insights into server and client performance metrics, including RPC statistics, read and write operations, and error counts.

Setting up an NFS server is a foundational task that enables efficient, centralized data sharing across networked systems. When properly configured with attention to security, performance, and access controls, an NFS server becomes a powerful component of any IT infrastructure, supporting collaborative workflows, application hosting, and storage consolidation across a wide range of use cases.

Configuring NFS Clients

Configuring NFS clients is a critical step in enabling seamless access to shared directories that are exported by an NFS server. The client-side setup ensures that remote file systems are properly integrated into the local file system hierarchy of the client machine, allowing users and applications to interact with remote data as if it were stored locally. The configuration process involves installing the necessary software, mounting the remote NFS shares, fine-tuning mount options, and implementing measures for security and performance optimization.

The first requirement in configuring an NFS client is to install the NFS client software package. Most modern UNIX-like operating systems, such as Linux, BSD variants, or Solaris, include a package that provides the NFS client utilities. On Linux systems, this package is typically called nfs-common or nfs-utils, depending on the distribution. This package contains the tools and libraries needed to initiate connections to NFS servers, perform mount operations, and handle NFS communication over the network.

Once the necessary package is installed, the client system can proceed to mount the NFS share provided by the server. The most common method is to use the mount command, specifying the type as nfs, the remote server's address, the exported directory, and the local mount point where the share will be accessible. For instance, a typical command might look like mount -t nfs 192.168.1.10:/srv/nfs/projects /mnt/projects, where 192.168.1.10 is the server IP address, /srv/nfs/projects is the exported directory on the server, and /mnt/projects is the directory on the client where the NFS share will be mounted.

Before issuing the mount command, the local mount point must exist on the client system. This requires creating the directory, such as /mnt/projects, using the mkdir command. Once mounted, the client can access files and directories on the NFS share as if they were part of the local file system. Applications and users will see no difference between working with files locally or across the NFS mount, thanks to NFS's transparency.

To ensure the NFS share persists across system reboots, administrators should configure an entry in the client's /etc/fstab file. The fstab entry typically includes the server address, the exported directory, the mount point, the file system type (nfs or nfs4), and mount options. For example, a simple fstab entry might look like 192.168.1.10:/srv/nfs/projects /mnt/projects nfs defaults 0 0. When properly configured, this entry ensures that the NFS share is automatically mounted each time the system boots.

Mount options play a vital role in controlling how the client interacts with the NFS server. These options affect performance, reliability, and security. One of the most fundamental options is the choice between hard and soft mounts. A hard mount causes the client to retry indefinitely if the server becomes unresponsive, ensuring that applications eventually regain access to the NFS share once the server is available again. A soft mount, on the other hand, allows the client to give up after a specified number of retries, which prevents system hangs but may result in file operation failures.

Other important mount options include rsize and wsize, which control the size of read and write buffers. By default, these values are often set automatically based on the server's capabilities, but administrators can manually adjust them to optimize performance based on network conditions and workload characteristics. Larger buffer sizes can improve throughput over high-latency networks but may consume more memory, while smaller buffer sizes can reduce memory usage but might limit transfer speeds.

The timeo and retrans options configure the timeout and retry behavior of NFS client requests. Timeo defines the amount of time the client waits before retrying a failed request, while retrans determines how many times the client retries before giving up (in the case of soft mounts) or continuing indefinitely (in the case of hard mounts). Properly tuning these settings is especially important for clients operating over wide area networks or in environments where the NFS server might experience temporary outages.

NFS clients also benefit from attribute and data caching mechanisms to reduce the number of remote calls to the server and improve performance. The actimeo option controls how long file attributes are cached before they are refreshed from the server. Similarly, noac disables attribute caching entirely, ensuring that each file operation fetches fresh metadata from the server. While disabling caching may improve data consistency in multi-client environments, it comes at the cost of increased network traffic and reduced performance.

For environments using NFSv4, it is common to configure mounts with the nfs4 type instead of nfs, which defaults to earlier versions. NFSv4 introduces features such as integrated locking, improved security, and better firewall compatibility by consolidating operations on a single TCP port. NFSv4 also provides support for Access Control Lists (ACLs), enabling finer-grained permissions management when interacting with files on the server.

Security considerations are paramount when configuring NFS clients, especially in environments that operate over untrusted networks. NFSv4 supports Kerberos-based authentication, providing strong protection against unauthorized access. To use Kerberos with NFSv4, the client system must be joined to the same Kerberos realm as the server and configured to obtain Kerberos tickets before accessing the NFS share. The rpc.gssd daemon is responsible for managing Kerberos credentials on the client and facilitating secure communication with the server.

In addition to Kerberos, clients should adhere to best practices such as limiting access to NFS shares via firewall rules and using VPN tunnels or encrypted networks when sharing files over untrusted connections. Careful export configurations on the server side, combined with proper client-side authentication and network restrictions, help mitigate the risk of unauthorized data access.

Automounting NFS shares on demand is another client configuration option that can enhance flexibility and reduce resource usage. The autofs service enables the dynamic mounting and unmounting of NFS shares based on usage. When a user or application accesses a predefined directory, autofs triggers the mount operation automatically. After a period of inactivity, autofs unmounts the share to conserve system resources. This approach is particularly useful in environments where many NFS shares exist, but only a subset is accessed at any given time.

Once the client is configured and the NFS share is mounted, administrators should verify the setup by performing basic file operations such as creating directories, writing test files, and reading existing data. Tools like df -h can confirm that the NFS share is properly mounted and providing the expected amount of storage space. Administrators can also use nfsstat on the client to gather statistics about NFS operations and performance metrics.

Monitoring the client's system logs is another important aspect of maintenance. Logs related to NFS activity are typically located in /var/log/messages or /var/log/syslog and can reveal useful information about mount issues, network problems, or file access errors. Staying vigilant to these messages ensures that potential issues are detected and resolved promptly.

Configuring an NFS client is a straightforward but crucial step in leveraging the full benefits of NFS file sharing. With the proper combination of mount options, caching strategies, and security configurations, clients can efficiently and securely access shared directories across the network, supporting collaborative workflows and centralized data management in a variety of computing environments.

NFS Exports and Access Control

At the heart of every NFS server is the ability to export directories, making them accessible to remote clients across the network. Exports are the mechanism through which an NFS server shares portions of its file system, allowing other systems to mount and interact with these shared directories as if they were part of the client's local file hierarchy. Configuring exports properly is essential for balancing accessibility, performance, and security. Without carefully defined exports and access control, an NFS server may expose sensitive data or become vulnerable to misuse or unauthorized access.

The primary configuration file for NFS exports is /etc/exports. This file defines which directories will be shared, the specific clients or networks permitted to access them, and the rules governing their interaction with the exported directories. Each line in the /etc/exports file corresponds to a single export and contains three critical components: the directory to export, the client specifications, and the export options. For example, an entry might look like /srv/nfs/public 192.168.1.0/24(rw,sync,no_root_squash), where /srv/nfs/public is the directory being shared, 192.168.1.0/24 specifies the network allowed access, and rw,sync,no_root_squash are the access control and behavior options applied to that export.

One of the most fundamental access control measures is restricting which clients or networks are allowed to mount and access the export. This is done by specifying client IP addresses, hostnames, or entire network subnets in the /etc/exports file. By limiting access to trusted networks or specific hosts, administrators can minimize the attack surface and reduce the risk of unauthorized connections. For example, specifying a single IP address like 192.168.1.100 or a hostname like client1.example.com restricts access to a specific client, while specifying a subnet like 192.168.1.0/24 grants access to all hosts within that subnet.

The export options following the client specification are critical in determining the behavior of the NFS share. One of the most commonly used options is rw, which grants clients read and write access to the exported directory. Alternatively, the ro option can be used to enforce read-only access, preventing clients from making changes to the shared data. The choice between rw and ro depends on the intended use case and security requirements. For example, directories containing application binaries or public datasets might be exported as read-only to prevent accidental or malicious modifications.

Another important option is sync, which dictates that changes made by clients are committed to stable storage on the server before the server responds to the client. This ensures data integrity, especially in the event of a server crash, but may impact performance. The async option allows the server to acknowledge write requests before the data is physically written to disk, improving performance but introducing a small risk of data loss under certain conditions.

The root_squash and no_root_squash options control how the server handles requests from the root user on client systems. By default, NFS implements root squashing, which maps the root user from the client to a less privileged user, typically nfsnobody, on the server. This prevents the client's root user from bypassing file system permissions and accessing or modifying files they should not be able to. Root squashing is a critical security measure and is generally recommended for most environments. However, there are situations, such as trusted internal networks or certain system administration workflows, where no_root_squash may be used to allow client root users to retain their privileges on the server. This option should be applied cautiously, as it can expose the server to potential privilege escalation risks.

The all_squash option is another export setting that forces all users from the client, regardless of their user ID, to be mapped to the anonymous user on the server. This is often used for public read-only exports or in environments where fine-grained permission control is unnecessary or undesirable.

User and group identity mapping between the client and server is a critical aspect of NFS access control. NFS relies on the consistency of numeric user and group IDs between systems. If a user has UID 1000 on the client but a different UID on the server, permission mismatches can occur, leading to access issues or unintended privilege escalation. In managed environments, administrators typically use centralized identity management solutions such as LDAP or NIS to ensure that user and group IDs are consistent across all systems. Alternatively, manual synchronization of /etc/passwd and /etc/group files can be performed, though this is more prone to errors in large environments.

Beyond basic access control, NFS supports additional options to refine client behavior and improve resilience. The subtree_check option enables the server to verify that file requests are within the boundaries of the exported directory, adding a layer of protection against directory traversal attacks. Disabling this check with no_subtree_check can improve performance, especially when exporting subdirectories of large file systems, but may reduce security in certain configurations.

For environments using NFSv4, the traditional /etc/exports file is still used, but NFSv4 introduces enhancements such as support for Access Control Lists (ACLs). Unlike the simple owner-group-other permission model of traditional UNIX systems, ACLs allow administrators to define more granular permissions on files and directories, specifying different levels of access for multiple users and groups. NFSv4 ACLs can be managed using tools such as nfs4_setfacl and nfs4_getfacl, providing a more flexible permission model for complex environments.

In addition to export-level controls, NFS servers can implement firewall rules and TCP wrapper configurations to restrict incoming traffic to NFS-related ports from trusted networks. Combining export controls with network-layer filtering provides a defense-in-depth approach to securing NFS shares. This is especially important when operating in hybrid environments where NFS shares may be accessed across different subnets or routed networks.

Export configurations should be revisited regularly as part of standard server maintenance routines. Changes in network architecture, evolving security policies, or shifting organizational requirements might necessitate updates to existing exports. Administrators should ensure that unnecessary exports are removed or disabled and that overly permissive options are tightened to align with security best practices.

After editing the /etc/exports file, changes can be applied without restarting the NFS service by running exportfs -ra. This command re-reads the configuration and updates the active exports, minimizing service disruption. Administrators can also use exportfs -v to verify the active export list and confirm that access control settings have been applied correctly.

NFS exports and access control form the foundation of secure and efficient file sharing in NFS environments. By carefully configuring export rules, limiting client access, and selecting appropriate export options, administrators can create a balanced NFS deployment that meets performance expectations while minimizing security risks. This fine-tuned control over shared directories is what enables NFS to serve as a reliable and flexible solution for distributed data access in networks of all sizes.

NFS Mount Options Explained

Mount options in NFS are critical for defining how a client connects to and interacts with an NFS server's exported file systems. These options influence everything from performance and reliability to data consistency and fault tolerance. Selecting the right combination of mount options ensures that the client's interaction with the remote file system is aligned with the environment's operational and security requirements. Understanding these options is essential for system administrators aiming to optimize NFS for specific workloads, network conditions, and use cases.

One of the most fundamental mount options is the distinction between hard and soft mounts. A hard mount instructs the client to retry requests to the NFS server indefinitely if the server becomes unavailable. This ensures that applications dependent on NFS-mounted directories will eventually regain access once the server is back online. It is the preferred option for critical data where the risk of data corruption or incomplete transactions due to dropped connections must be minimized. A soft mount, on the other hand, allows the client to give up after a specified number of retries or a timeout. While this prevents the client system from becoming unresponsive during server outages, it may result in application errors or incomplete file operations, making it more suitable for non-critical or read-only mounts where availability interruptions are less consequential.

The timeo and retrans options work alongside hard and soft mounts to control how the client handles timeouts and retries. The timeo option specifies the timeout value in tenths of a second before the client retries a request. For example, a timeo=30 setting results in a 3-second timeout before a retry is attempted. The retrans option defines how many times a request is retried before the client takes further action, such as reporting an error or continuing to retry indefinitely in the case of a hard mount. Fine-tuning timeo and retrans can help balance responsiveness and reliability, particularly over unreliable or high-latency networks.

Another pair of important options are rsize and wsize, which determine the maximum size of read and write requests that the client will send to the server. These values are specified in bytes and are often automatically negotiated based on the server's capabilities and network conditions. However, administrators may choose to manually set rsize and wsize to optimize performance. Larger block sizes, such as 65536 bytes, can reduce the number of RPC calls required for large file transfers, improving throughput on fast and stable networks. Conversely, smaller sizes may be appropriate for networks with higher error rates or where memory consumption must be minimized.

The intr option, relevant to hard mounts, allows NFS requests to be interrupted if a user sends an interrupt signal such as CTRL+C. Without the intr option, a client may hang indefinitely during an NFS server outage, with no way for users to abort the blocked process. This can lead to system unresponsiveness, particularly in interactive sessions. While intr was more commonly used in earlier NFS versions, modern NFS clients often treat interrupts more gracefully, but administrators may still encounter this option in legacy systems.

The bg option is another useful setting, particularly when dealing with remote or unreliable servers. It instructs the client to attempt to mount the NFS share in the background if the initial mount attempt fails. This prevents mount failures from blocking system boot processes or delaying service start-ups, which is critical in environments where NFS servers may be unavailable during certain times or network conditions are unpredictable.

Caching-related mount options play a crucial role in performance and consistency. The actimeo option sets the attribute cache timeout, defining how long file metadata such as ownership, permissions, and modification times are cached on the client before being revalidated with the server. This can improve performance by reducing metadata-related RPC traffic but may lead to stale data if multiple clients are actively modifying shared files. A low actimeo value ensures fresher metadata at the cost of increased network traffic.

The noac option disables attribute caching entirely, forcing the client to fetch metadata directly from the server for each file operation. While this ensures the highest level of consistency, it can dramatically degrade performance, especially in high-latency or high-throughput environments. The choice between enabling or disabling attribute caching depends heavily on the workload. For example, in shared development environments where multiple users or automated processes modify files concurrently, disabling caching might prevent race conditions or conflicts.

The tcp and udp options specify the transport protocol used for NFS communication. While older versions of NFS supported UDP due to its low overhead in LAN environments, modern best practices favor TCP, which offers reliable data delivery and improved performance over WANs or lossy networks. Most contemporary NFS clients default to TCP, but specifying tcp explicitly can help ensure consistent behavior across different systems or distributions.

In NFSv4, the sec option becomes particularly important for defining the security model of the NFS session. Options such as sec=sys use the standard UNIX authentication model, relying on client-side user and group IDs for permission enforcement. More secure configurations, such as sec=krb5, enable Kerberos authentication, while sec=krb5i and sec=krb5p add integrity and privacy protections by providing checksums or encrypting the NFS traffic, respectively. These options are essential in environments that require compliance with security standards or where data is transmitted over untrusted networks.

The nolock option disables file locking on the client, which may be necessary in certain scenarios where file locking is handled by alternative mechanisms or when accessing read-only exports. However, disabling locking in environments where concurrent file access occurs can lead to data corruption or inconsistent file states, so this option should be applied judiciously.

Another option that administrators encounter is vers, which specifies the version of the NFS protocol to be used. For example, vers=3 forces the client to use NFSv3, while vers=4 ensures NFSv4 is used. In environments where backward compatibility with legacy systems is required, explicitly setting the version helps avoid protocol negotiation mismatches and compatibility issues.

The lookupcache option in NFSv4 controls how aggressively directory entries are cached by the client. Options like lookupcache=none disable directory entry caching entirely, while lookupcache=positive caches only successful lookups, and lookupcache=all enables full caching. Tuning this option can help balance directory lookup performance with the need for data consistency in rapidly changing directories.

For automated environments, the soft, bg, and retry options are often combined to ensure non-blocking mount behavior. For instance, configuring a mount with soft,bg,retry=5 allows the system to attempt mounting the NFS share in the background and stop after five unsuccessful retries, preventing indefinite hangs during boot or service start-up.

By understanding and applying these mount options strategically, system administrators can tailor NFS client behavior to meet specific performance, availability, and security goals. Whether operating in a tightly controlled enterprise network or an open, multi-user environment with varying workloads, the ability to fine-tune how NFS clients mount and interact with shared directories is vital to achieving stable and efficient distributed file access.

NFS over TCP vs. UDP

The Network File System, like many protocols built on Remote Procedure Call (RPC), relies on an underlying transport layer to carry its communication between clients and servers. For most of its history, NFS has supported both the Transmission Control Protocol (TCP) and the User Datagram Protocol (UDP) as transport mechanisms. Each protocol has distinct characteristics that impact performance, reliability, and suitability depending on the network environment. Understanding the differences between using NFS over TCP versus UDP is key to optimizing file-sharing behavior in a wide variety of deployment scenarios.

In its earliest implementations, NFS was designed to work primarily over UDP. At the time, networks were typically local area networks (LANs) with low latency, minimal packet loss, and simple topologies. UDP, being a connectionless and lightweight protocol, was favored for its lower overhead compared to TCP. By avoiding the need for connection establishment and teardown, flow control, and retransmission mechanisms, UDP allowed NFS to process file system operations quickly, resulting in fast response times. The simplicity of UDP contributed to reduced CPU consumption on both client and server systems, making it an efficient option for smaller, localized network environments where reliability could largely be assumed.

However, UDP's lack of reliability features also introduced significant limitations. Since UDP does not guarantee packet delivery, order, or data integrity, the burden of handling packet retransmissions and session management fell entirely on the NFS protocol itself, which was originally designed to be stateless. In an ideal, congestion-free LAN, these limitations were manageable, but as networks grew larger and more complex, with increased latency and potential for packet loss, UDP-based NFS encountered noticeable performance degradation. In wide area networks (WANs) or networks with high traffic levels, dropped packets, and the subsequent need for retransmissions by the NFS layer, could cause significant slowdowns and inconsistencies in file operations.

Recognizing these challenges, later versions of NFS introduced and increasingly favored TCP as the preferred transport protocol. Unlike UDP, TCP is a connection-oriented protocol that provides reliable data delivery, in-order transmission, flow control, and congestion management. When using TCP, NFS offloads much of the responsibility for handling lost packets and ensuring reliable communication to the transport layer. This greatly improves performance and stability in environments with higher latencies, larger distances between clients and servers, or more frequent network disruptions.

TCP's ability to segment data into manageable chunks and automatically retransmit lost segments without involving the application layer is particularly advantageous for NFS. File transfers over TCP are generally smoother and less prone to interruption or corruption, especially when transferring large files or operating in networks with occasional packet loss. Moreover, TCP's flow control mechanisms help prevent network congestion by dynamically adjusting transmission rates based on network conditions. This adaptive behavior is absent in UDP, which can exacerbate network congestion by continuing to transmit packets at a fixed rate regardless of the network's current state.

As NFS evolved, particularly with the release of NFS version 3 and beyond, TCP became increasingly recognized as the more robust transport for distributed file systems. While NFSv3 still allowed for both TCP and UDP, most production environments began migrating to TCP to capitalize on its reliability and better handling of adverse network conditions. By the time NFSv4 was introduced, TCP was mandated as the default transport protocol. This shift marked a significant milestone in NFS's evolution, streamlining firewall configurations, improving security, and reducing operational complexity.

In addition to reliability, TCP offered improvements in data integrity. Since TCP provides checksumming at the transport layer, the likelihood of corrupted data going unnoticed between client and server is substantially lower than with UDP, which leaves error detection and correction entirely to the application layer or dependent systems. For mission-critical applications where data accuracy is paramount, this built-in integrity checking provided by TCP became an indispensable benefit.

Despite the clear advantages of TCP in modern networks, there are still niche scenarios where UDP might be considered. In extremely low-latency LAN environments with minimal interference and very high-performance requirements, UDP's lower overhead could theoretically yield faster response times for certain workloads. However, such environments are rare today, and even in these cases, the performance gains are often marginal compared to the potential stability benefits offered by TCP.

Another consideration when comparing NFS over TCP and UDP is related to firewall and network security configurations. Because UDP-based NFS requires multiple daemons operating on dynamic ports, it can complicate firewall rule sets and network segmentation policies. TCP simplifies this by consolidating communication onto a single, well-known port (2049) for NFSv4, making it easier to implement secure and predictable network access controls. This reduction in complexity aligns well with modern security practices, where minimizing the number of open ports and simplifying firewall rules is a key objective.

From a troubleshooting perspective, TCP also provides benefits through its verbose session management and logging capabilities. Administrators analyzing packet captures or system logs can more easily trace connection issues, retransmissions, and congestion control behaviors in TCP streams compared to the stateless nature of UDP, which lacks such feedback mechanisms.

When choosing between TCP and UDP for NFS deployments, administrators must consider the nature of their network infrastructure. In legacy systems or highly controlled LAN environments where UDP is already in place and performing adequately, administrators may opt to maintain UDP for simplicity and consistency. However, in most modern enterprise and cloud environments, where networks are inherently more complex and distributed, TCP has become the default and recommended choice.

Additionally, certain advanced NFS features, such as file delegations, stateful locking, and Kerberos-based security found in NFSv4, are tightly coupled with the reliability and state management capabilities that TCP provides. These features depend on maintaining consistent and uninterrupted sessions, making TCP not only a performance choice but also a functional necessity.

Ultimately, while NFS originally leveraged UDP to serve its early design philosophy of statelessness and low overhead in simple networks, the widespread shift to TCP has brought stability, efficiency, and robustness to modern NFS deployments. The evolution from UDP to TCP reflects the broader trend of adapting legacy protocols to meet the demands of more distributed, larger-scale, and security-conscious network environments. The decision to use TCP or UDP should always be aligned with the specific operational characteristics of the deployment, but in most cases, TCP's advantages now make it the transport of choice for NFS in contemporary infrastructures.

Securing NFS: Best Practices

Securing NFS is a critical aspect of deploying this protocol in production environments, especially as modern networks have expanded beyond simple local area networks into complex, hybrid, and sometimes public-facing infrastructures. While NFS was originally designed for trusted LAN environments where security concerns were minimal, today's threats and compliance requirements demand that administrators implement a layered security approach to protect sensitive data, prevent unauthorized access, and ensure integrity across the NFS ecosystem.

The first step in securing NFS begins at the export level. The /etc/exports file is where administrators define which directories will be shared and which clients or networks are allowed access. Limiting access to specific IP addresses, subnets, or hostnames is essential in reducing the attack surface. Open-ended exports that allow universal access, such as exporting directories to *, can expose the server to unnecessary risks, especially in environments where NFS traffic may traverse untrusted networks. Instead, each export should be as restrictive as possible, specifying only the known and trusted clients that require access to the shared resource.

Export options also provide additional security mechanisms. The root_squash option is a fundamental defense that prevents root users on client machines from having root privileges on the NFS server. When enabled, this option maps client-side root requests to the anonymous user (often nfsnobody), effectively limiting what the root user can do on shared directories. While no_root_squash can be useful in certain controlled environments, it introduces a substantial security risk if used improperly. For shared resources that need to be protected from administrative-level interference from clients, keeping root_squash enabled is a best practice.

The choice between read-only and read-write exports also plays a key role in securing NFS. Exports that only require read access, such as those used for serving application binaries or public data, should be explicitly configured with the ro option to prevent clients from modifying data. On the other hand, rw exports should be limited to only those clients that require write access, ensuring that modification privileges are restricted to trusted systems and users.

A critical component of securing NFS is implementing network-layer security controls. NFS relies on several network services, including rpcbind, rpc.mountd, and nfsd, which by default may use dynamically assigned ports. These ports should be locked down using firewalls to restrict access to only trusted IP ranges. Modern firewalls can be configured to allow traffic on TCP port 2049, which is used by NFSv4, while also limiting access to rpcbind and other auxiliary services. The principle of least privilege applies here as well, meaning only the minimum necessary services and ports should be exposed to the network.

Encrypting NFS traffic is another critical consideration, particularly when NFS traffic crosses network boundaries, such as in WAN environments or between data centers. By default, NFS does not encrypt data in transit, making it vulnerable to packet sniffing and man-in-the-middle attacks. To address this, administrators can deploy NFSv4 with Kerberos authentication and encryption. Kerberos provides mutual authentication between client and server, ensuring that both parties are legitimate before establishing a session. Using Kerberos with integrity (krb5i) or privacy (krb5p) ensures that data is not only authenticated but also optionally encrypted to protect against eavesdropping.

Setting up Kerberos with NFS requires integrating the NFS server and clients into the same Kerberos realm and configuring service principals for secure authentication. The rpc.gssd and rpc.svcgssd daemons are necessary for handling Kerberos credentials and ensuring secure session management. While this setup can be more complex than standard UNIX authentication, it significantly enhances security and is highly recommended for sensitive environments where regulatory compliance or data protection is a concern.

Another best practice is to disable unused NFS protocol versions. Older versions of NFS, such as NFSv2, lack essential security features, including proper locking, strong authentication mechanisms, and TCP-only communication. By disabling support for outdated protocol versions, administrators can reduce the risk of exploitation through known vulnerabilities. Modern servers should default to NFSv4, which integrates improved security features and simplifies firewall configurations by consolidating communication to a single port.

Administrators should also consider disabling anonymous user access when it is not strictly necessary. By default, NFS may map unknown users to the nfsnobody account, which could allow unauthorized users to read from or write to exports depending on file system permissions. Explicitly setting the all_squash and anonuid/anongid options in /etc/exports can control how anonymous users are mapped and what permissions they have on the shared directories.

Securing the underlying file system is equally important. Even with carefully crafted export configurations, the server's local file system permissions act as the final gatekeeper. Ensuring that directories and files have the appropriate UNIX permissions limits what users and services can do once they access an export. Regular audits of file permissions, ownership, and access controls help identify and correct overly permissive settings that could expose sensitive data.

Logging and monitoring are vital components of NFS security. System logs, often located in /var/log/messages or /var/log/syslog, provide insight into NFS activity, including successful and failed mount attempts, file access patterns, and daemon restarts. Tools like auditd can extend logging capabilities to track specific file-level operations, generating audit trails that are invaluable for compliance and incident response purposes. Regularly reviewing logs helps detect unauthorized access attempts, misconfigurations, or unusual patterns that could indicate a compromise.

For additional protection, administrators can integrate intrusion detection systems (IDS) or intrusion prevention systems (IPS) to monitor NFS traffic for suspicious behavior. Combined with firewall and logging mechanisms, these tools provide an extra layer of defense against threats such as brute force attempts, denial-of-service attacks, or lateral movement within the network.

In environments with high availability requirements, NFS servers may also be part of larger clustered file systems or networked storage platforms. In such cases, securing the entire storage stack is essential. This includes ensuring that the underlying network infrastructure is segmented properly, management interfaces are secured, and storage nodes are hardened according to industry best practices.

Maintaining an up-to-date NFS server is a fundamental step in securing the service. Regularly applying patches and security updates ensures that vulnerabilities in the NFS daemons, underlying operating system, or kernel-level NFS modules are mitigated. Automated update management tools or centralized configuration management systems can help enforce consistent security policies and software versions across large-scale NFS deployments.

Training users and system administrators on security awareness is also a valuable practice. Ensuring that users understand how NFS authentication, permissions, and mounts work reduces the likelihood of accidental exposure or misuse of shared directories. Establishing clear policies around acceptable use, mount configurations, and export restrictions contributes to a culture of security-conscious operations.

By combining strict export configurations, secure transport mechanisms, robust authentication, and diligent system monitoring, NFS can be deployed as a secure and reliable file-sharing solution, even in environments where security is paramount. Implementing these best practices ensures that data integrity and confidentiality are maintained while supporting the high-performance and collaborative workflows that NFS was designed to facilitate.

NFS Performance Tuning

Optimizing the performance of an NFS deployment is essential for ensuring that file sharing over the network meets the expectations of users and applications. Without proper tuning, NFS may suffer from slow response times, latency issues, or bottlenecks, particularly under heavy loads or in distributed environments. Tuning NFS for optimal performance requires attention to multiple layers, including network parameters, server and client configurations, and the underlying storage infrastructure. Each element plays a crucial role in how efficiently data is transferred between NFS clients and servers.

One of the first areas to consider in NFS performance tuning is the configuration of read and write buffer sizes. The rsize and wsize options define the maximum size of NFS read and write operations, respectively. These settings control how much data is transferred in a single RPC call between the client and the server. Larger values, such as 65536 bytes or higher depending on the system's capabilities, reduce the number of RPC calls required to read or write large files, thus lowering the overhead associated with processing many small requests. However, these buffer sizes must be supported by both the client and the server, as well as the network infrastructure, to realize performance benefits. In high-bandwidth, low-latency environments, increasing rsize and wsize can significantly improve throughput.

Caching is another critical factor in improving NFS performance. On the client side, NFS employs attribute and data caching mechanisms to reduce the frequency of remote calls to the server. The actimeo option controls how long file attributes are cached before they are revalidated with the server. Setting actimeo to a higher value reduces the number of metadata-related RPC requests, which is beneficial in read-heavy workloads where file system metadata does not change frequently. However, in environments where files are modified by multiple clients, longer cache timeouts can lead to stale data and inconsistencies. Finding the right balance between cache duration and consistency is essential. In workloads that require strong consistency, options like noac, which disables attribute caching, might be necessary, although they come at the cost of additional network traffic and reduced performance.

The choice between synchronous and asynchronous writes has a significant impact on NFS performance. Synchronous writes, enforced by the sync export option, require that data is physically written to disk before an acknowledgment is sent to the client. While this approach ensures a higher level of data integrity, it can slow down write operations, particularly when dealing with storage devices that have slower input/output capabilities. The async option, on the other hand, allows the server to acknowledge writes before the data has been committed to disk, providing a performance boost but with a slight risk of data loss in the event of a server crash. In environments where performance is prioritized and the risk is acceptable or mitigated through other means like redundant storage or battery-backed write caches, using async can help improve overall write throughput.

On the server side, tuning the number of nfsd threads is another method for enhancing performance. The nfsd daemon handles incoming client requests, and increasing the number of nfsd threads allows the server to process more simultaneous requests. This is especially important in environments where many clients are accessing the NFS server concurrently. The optimal number of threads depends on the server's hardware capabilities and the expected workload. On most Linux systems, the number of threads can be adjusted by modifying the nfs.conf configuration file or by using system-specific commands such as nfsdcount. Increasing thread counts beyond what the CPU can handle effectively, however, can lead to diminishing returns or resource contention, so careful testing is required.

Network tuning is equally important when optimizing NFS performance. NFS over TCP benefits from tuning kernel-level TCP parameters on both the client and server. Adjusting the size of the TCP window using sysctl parameters like net.core.rmem_max and net.core.wmem_max can help accommodate larger rsize and wsize values, improving performance over high-latency or high-bandwidth networks. Similarly, increasing the maximum number of file descriptors available to the NFS server process ensures that it can handle large numbers of open file handles, which is critical in environments where clients frequently open and close files or maintain long-lived sessions.

The use of jumbo frames is another network-level optimization that can benefit NFS performance. By default, Ethernet frames carry a maximum payload of 1500 bytes. Enabling jumbo frames allows larger payloads, often up to 9000 bytes, reducing the number of frames required to transmit large blocks of data. Jumbo frames are particularly beneficial in storage networks or high-performance computing environments where large files are frequently transferred. However, all devices in the network path, including switches, routers, and network interface cards, must support and be configured for jumbo frames for this optimization to be effective.

For NFSv4 and later, enabling and tuning delegations can also yield performance benefits. Delegations allow the server to grant exclusive access to certain files or file attributes to clients, reducing the need for repeated client-server communications. Delegations are particularly effective in workloads where clients work with specific files in isolation from other clients. However, in highly collaborative environments where multiple clients access the same files simultaneously, delegations may provide limited benefit and can be disabled if necessary.

The use of parallel NFS (pNFS), introduced in NFSv4.1, provides another layer of performance enhancement for large-scale environments. pNFS decouples metadata and data access, allowing clients to retrieve metadata from a metadata server while accessing actual file data directly from storage servers in parallel. This approach significantly improves scalability and throughput by avoiding metadata bottlenecks and distributing data access across multiple nodes. Implementing pNFS, however, requires compatible storage infrastructure and careful configuration to fully realize its performance potential.

Tuning NFS client mount options is equally critical for maximizing performance. Mount options like tcp, hard, and intr should be carefully selected based on the application's requirements and the network conditions. TCP is preferred in most modern environments due to its reliability and better performance over WANs. Hard mounts ensure persistent retries in case of server unavailability, while intr allows administrators or users to interrupt NFS-related operations if necessary, preventing system hangs during outages.

Finally, administrators should monitor NFS server and client performance regularly using tools such as nfsstat, iostat, vmstat, and netstat. These tools provide valuable insights into metrics like RPC request rates, read and write throughput, disk I/O latency, and network utilization. Continuous performance monitoring helps identify bottlenecks, whether they originate at the network layer, in storage subsystems, or in client-server communication. By analyzing these metrics, administrators can fine-tune system parameters and adjust configurations to maintain optimal performance as workloads evolve and infrastructure scales.

NFS performance tuning is a holistic process that involves coordinating adjustments across storage, network, server, and client layers. By applying thoughtful configurations and regularly reviewing performance data, administrators can ensure that NFS continues to deliver efficient, reliable, and high-performing file-sharing capabilities across a variety of deployment scenarios.

Understanding NFS Caching

Caching is a fundamental component of the Network File System, playing a crucial role in enhancing performance and reducing the load on both NFS servers and network infrastructure. At its core, caching allows clients to temporarily store data and metadata locally, minimizing the need to repeatedly fetch information from the server. While caching can significantly boost read and write performance, it also introduces challenges related to data consistency, especially in multi-client environments where the same files may be accessed and modified concurrently. Understanding how NFS implements caching and how it impacts system behavior is key to optimizing file system performance without compromising data integrity.

NFS caching primarily occurs on the client side, where the NFS client module within the operating system manages local caches for file data, directory entries, and file attributes. This means that when a client application reads a file from an NFS-mounted directory, the data is first fetched from the server and then stored in the client's local memory or cache. If the application subsequently accesses the same file, the request may be satisfied directly from the client's cache, avoiding the need to send another read request to the server. This local caching mechanism is highly effective in reducing network traffic and improving response times, especially in read-heavy workloads where the same data is accessed repeatedly.

NFS employs several distinct types of caches to optimize performance. The attribute cache stores metadata about files, including permissions, ownership, file sizes, and modification timestamps. By caching these attributes, the client avoids querying the server every time it needs to display file listings or check file properties. The directory entry cache, or dentry cache, stores information about directory structures and file locations within directories, accelerating directory traversals and file lookups. Finally, the data cache stores the actual contents of files, enabling fast access to file data without network latency.

The duration for which cached information is considered valid is controlled by a series of timers and caching policies. The actimeo mount option, for example, sets a common timeout for attribute caching, specifying how long attributes remain valid before the client revalidates them with the server. This value can usually be specified in seconds and can range from very short durations to longer periods depending on the use case. For systems where file metadata changes infrequently and performance is a priority, a higher actimeo value may be appropriate. In contrast, in collaborative environments where multiple clients frequently modify shared files, a lower actimeo value helps maintain consistency by forcing more frequent server checks.

In addition to actimeo, NFS provides the acdirmin and acdirmax options to define minimum and maximum durations for which directory attributes are cached, and acregmin and acregmax to control the caching of regular file attributes. These parameters provide finer control over how aggressively or conservatively the client caches file system metadata. Tuning these values is often a balancing act, as longer caching durations reduce server load and improve client-side performance but increase the likelihood of clients working with stale metadata.

NFS data caching can also be influenced by the choice of mount options such as noac, which disables attribute caching entirely. When noac is enabled, every file operation results in direct communication with the server to retrieve the latest metadata. While this guarantees strong consistency and is useful in environments where multiple clients frequently access and modify shared files, it also places a higher load on the server and increases network traffic, leading to degraded performance.

The FS-Cache subsystem on Linux offers an additional layer of caching for NFS clients. FS-Cache allows NFS clients to cache files on local disk storage rather than relying solely on in-memory caching. This is especially valuable in environments with large datasets or clients with limited RAM resources. By caching files on disk, FS-Cache helps reduce repeated network access for large files and can be particularly effective in scenarios where clients frequently read the same data but cannot store it all in memory. FS-Cache integrates seamlessly with the NFS client and is transparent to applications.

Consistency models in NFS are influenced by caching behavior. NFS is designed to be a close-to-open consistency model, meaning that changes to files are typically flushed and made visible to other clients when a file is closed. When a client closes a file after writing to it, the NFS client module ensures that the data is committed to the server, and any subsequent open operation from another client will see the updated file. However, inconsistencies can occur if two clients read and write to the same file simultaneously without closing it. To mitigate such risks, applications may implement file locking mechanisms, either through NFS's advisory locking or mandatory locking in some scenarios, ensuring that only one client can modify a file at a time.

The server also plays a role in caching, particularly through the use of page caches and disk caches. Modern NFS servers cache frequently accessed data in memory, allowing for faster retrieval when multiple clients request the same file or directory. The effectiveness of the server's cache depends on available system memory, storage speed, and how often data changes. When combined with client-side caching, the result is a multi-layered caching system where both the server and the clients work to minimize disk I/O and network latency.

However, caching introduces complexities in environments where data consistency and integrity are paramount. For example, in clustered or distributed computing environments where multiple processes on different clients simultaneously modify shared files, caching policies must be carefully tuned to avoid stale data issues. This is why some high-performance computing environments or collaborative workflows disable or reduce caching to prioritize real-time consistency over raw performance.

In addition to controlling caching through mount options and system parameters, administrators should monitor cache performance using tools such as nfsstat and iostat. These tools provide insights into cache hit rates, RPC call frequencies, and network traffic patterns. High cache hit rates generally indicate efficient caching, while frequent cache invalidations or low hit rates may point to suboptimal cache configurations or workloads that require stronger consistency.

Ultimately, understanding NFS caching is about balancing performance and consistency based on workload characteristics. For static or read-heavy environments, aggressive caching can yield substantial performance gains. In contrast, for write-heavy or collaborative scenarios, reducing caching aggressiveness may be necessary to ensure data remains accurate and up to date across all clients. By carefully tuning caching settings, administrators can ensure that NFS deployments meet the demands of their specific applications while optimizing server resources and minimizing unnecessary network load.

NFS Locking Mechanisms

Locking mechanisms in NFS play a vital role in ensuring data consistency and preventing file corruption when multiple clients simultaneously access and modify shared files. Unlike local file systems, where locking is handled entirely within the operating system's kernel, NFS operates in a distributed environment where clients and servers are separate systems communicating over a network. This distributed nature introduces unique challenges that NFS locking mechanisms are designed to address. Without effective locking, concurrent writes from different clients could lead to unpredictable results, race conditions, or corrupted data.

In its earlier versions, such as NFSv2 and NFSv3, NFS was designed as a stateless protocol. Statelessness simplifies server design and improves resilience to crashes but complicates stateful operations like file locking. To resolve this, NFS relied on an auxiliary protocol, the Network Lock Manager (NLM), to provide file locking capabilities. The NLM operates as a separate service alongside the NFS server, enabling clients to request and manage locks on remote files. When a client wants to lock a file, it communicates with the NLM service running on the server. The server then grants or denies the lock based on the current state of the file and whether other clients have already locked it.

The NLM supports two primary types of locks: shared (or read) locks and exclusive (or write) locks. Shared locks allow multiple clients to read a file concurrently without interfering with each other, whereas exclusive locks ensure that only a single client can write to or modify the file at any given time. NLM locks are advisory, meaning that applications must explicitly request and honor the locks. If an application ignores locking conventions, it could still access and modify locked files, leading to potential conflicts. Therefore, the effectiveness of NLM-based locking relies on application-level cooperation.

The NLM also supports file range locking, allowing clients to lock specific byte ranges within a file rather than locking the entire file. This granularity is beneficial in applications where different clients operate on distinct sections of large files, such as databases or log processors. File range locking helps improve concurrency and performance by permitting more parallel access while still preventing overlapping writes that could corrupt data.

Because NLM is a separate service from the NFS server, it introduces additional network traffic and complexity. Furthermore, NLM has its limitations, particularly in environments where network interruptions or server crashes occur. To mitigate the risk of stale locks persisting after a client crashes or disconnects unexpectedly, NLM works in conjunction with another service called the status monitor daemon, or rpc.statd. This daemon tracks the state of NFS clients and helps reclaim locks that might otherwise be left dangling in the event of client or server failures.

The introduction of NFSv4 marked a significant evolution in locking mechanisms by integrating locking directly into the core protocol. Unlike NFSv3, which depends on the external NLM service, NFSv4 provides native support for stateful file locking, eliminating the need for separate daemons to manage locks. NFSv4 locking is more robust, offering mandatory enforcement by the server and built-in crash recovery mechanisms that automatically reclaim locks held by disconnected or failed clients. This integration simplifies deployment and reduces the risk of stale locks, making NFSv4 the preferred choice for environments where file locking is a critical requirement.

NFSv4 locking operates on a lease-based model, where clients acquire leases from the server when they open files. These leases grant clients certain rights, such as the ability to perform read or write operations on a file. Leases can also include delegation rights, allowing the server to grant a client temporary exclusive access to manage locks or cache data locally without frequent server coordination. Delegations improve performance in workloads where files are accessed by a single client for extended periods. When the server needs to revoke a delegation, it notifies the client, which is then responsible for returning the delegated rights and flushing any cached data.

The NFSv4 protocol also includes a sequence of lock-related operations that clients use to request and release locks. These operations include OPEN, LOCK, LOCKU (unlock), and CLOSE, forming a state machine that ensures file access is properly coordinated across clients. The stateful design of NFSv4 means that the server maintains lock records and lease information for each active client session, allowing for efficient handling of locks and improved fault tolerance compared to the stateless NLM approach.

Despite the advances in NFSv4 locking, challenges can still arise, particularly in highly concurrent environments. For instance, lock contention can occur when multiple clients attempt to access the same file or byte range simultaneously, resulting in delays or reduced throughput. Administrators and application developers must design workflows and file structures to minimize lock contention where possible. Techniques such as splitting data into smaller files, using file range locking instead of whole-file locks, or implementing application-level queuing mechanisms can help reduce contention and improve performance.

NFS locking mechanisms also introduce considerations for cluster-aware applications or systems. In distributed environments with multiple NFS servers behind a load balancer or within a clustered file system, it is essential to ensure that lock management is centralized and consistent across all nodes. This typically requires using a shared storage backend or a clustered NFS implementation to prevent situations where different servers have conflicting lock states.

Administrators can monitor NFS locking activity using tools like nfsstat, which provides statistics about lock operations, or by examining system logs for locking-related messages. Troubleshooting lock-related issues often involves identifying patterns of lock contention, tracking down clients that may not be releasing locks properly, or resolving stale locks that may persist due to network disruptions or client crashes.

File locking is a critical tool in maintaining data integrity and preventing file corruption in shared NFS environments. Whether using NLM in NFSv3 or the integrated stateful locking model in NFSv4, locking mechanisms ensure that concurrent file access occurs in an orderly and predictable manner. While locking introduces additional complexity and overhead, it is a necessary trade-off in environments where collaboration and simultaneous access to shared data are essential.

By understanding the distinctions between advisory and mandatory locking, whole-file and range locks, and stateless versus stateful implementations, administrators and developers can design more resilient and efficient NFS deployments. Ensuring proper application behavior and tuning server and client configurations to match workload requirements will further enhance the effectiveness of NFS locking mechanisms, safeguarding data integrity in distributed file systems.

Delegations in NFSv4

Delegations in NFSv4 are a sophisticated mechanism designed to enhance performance by reducing the need for repeated interactions between NFS clients and the server. As a key feature introduced with NFSv4, delegations allow the server to temporarily grant a client exclusive or near-exclusive rights to perform certain operations on a file, most notably read and write caching. By giving the client delegated control over file operations, the protocol reduces the frequency of lock checks, open and close calls, and cache validation requests that would otherwise require constant communication with the server. Delegations are particularly useful in environments where clients frequently access and modify the same files without contention from other clients.

At a high level, delegations serve to extend the client's autonomy when interacting with files, thereby improving the efficiency of client-side caching and reducing network latency. When a client opens a file via the NFSv4 protocol, the server may choose to grant a delegation to that client, depending on the file's current access pattern and server policy. If no other client has an open handle to the file or if the server anticipates that there will be minimal risk of concurrent access, it may assign the delegation. Once granted, the client can cache data and metadata related to the file more aggressively, knowing that no other client is expected to modify the file in the meantime.

There are two primary types of delegations in NFSv4: read delegations and write delegations. A read delegation allows a client to cache file data and attributes locally without consulting the server for read consistency checks. This means the client can satisfy subsequent read requests directly from its local cache, which significantly reduces the latency typically involved in network file system operations. Read delegations are most effective in workloads where files are frequently read but not modified by multiple clients, such as configuration files, reference datasets, or documentation repositories.

Write delegations provide a client with temporary exclusive rights to modify a file. With a write delegation in place, the client can perform write operations and cache the data locally without immediately synchronizing changes to the server. Instead, the client can defer writing changes to the server until the file is closed or the delegation is returned. This reduces the overhead associated with repeated remote write operations, making write delegations particularly beneficial in workloads where a single client performs multiple updates to a file before closing it, such as in batch processing applications or data logging systems.

While delegations offer clear performance advantages, they must be managed carefully to preserve data consistency in a distributed environment. NFSv4 includes mechanisms for the server to recall delegations if another client attempts to open the same file in a conflicting mode. For example, if Client A holds a read delegation for a file and Client B tries to open that file for writing, the server will issue a recall request to Client A. The client is then responsible for flushing any cached data to the server and returning the delegation before Client B's write request can proceed. This recall process ensures that data consistency is maintained across all clients.

Clients receiving delegation recalls must respond promptly to avoid delays in processing the conflicting client's request. If a client holding a delegation is unresponsive, for example due to a crash or network failure, the server will initiate a recovery process to reclaim the delegation. This process may involve timeout mechanisms and session recovery features that are part of the NFSv4 protocol. In environments where stability and fault tolerance are critical, delegations must be combined with robust failure detection and recovery strategies to prevent resource contention or data access delays.

Delegations are granted at the discretion of the NFSv4 server, which uses internal heuristics and policy configurations to determine when delegations are appropriate. The server evaluates factors such as current file usage patterns, client activity levels, and historical access trends to make these decisions. In highly contentious environments where multiple clients frequently access and modify the same files, the server may opt to limit or withhold delegations altogether to avoid excessive delegation recalls and the associated overhead.

In some cases, administrators may choose to disable delegations on the server to simplify configuration or avoid potential complications in collaborative workflows. Disabling delegations forces clients to revert to the standard open-to-close consistency model, where metadata and data caches are validated more frequently against the server. While this reduces the performance benefits associated with delegations, it can be desirable in environments where file access patterns are unpredictable or where third-party applications do not properly handle delegation recalls.

Delegations also interact with NFSv4's lease-based locking model. Clients that receive a delegation effectively acquire a lease on the file, allowing them to operate on it under the terms of the granted delegation. These leases must be renewed periodically to inform the server that the client is still active and capable of responding to recall requests. The lease renewal process happens in the background, typically as part of other NFS operations, ensuring that the server can detect unresponsive clients and initiate recovery if necessary.

From a performance perspective, delegations can lead to significant reductions in network round trips, lower server CPU load, and improved application responsiveness. Applications that perform repeated reads or writes to the same files benefit most from the caching efficiencies enabled by delegations. For example, a software build system that repeatedly accesses header files or a database engine that logs transactions to the same set of files can take advantage of read and write delegations to reduce the latency and network load associated with file operations.

NFSv4 clients can be configured to support delegations by default, and most modern NFS implementations handle delegation requests and recalls transparently. Administrators and developers rarely need to modify application code to benefit from delegations, as the functionality is integrated into the NFS client and kernel-level file system operations. However, for highly specialized applications, awareness of how delegations work can inform better file access strategies and workload design.

Administrators should also monitor delegation activity using diagnostic tools such as nfsstat, which provides statistics on delegation grants, recalls, and returns. Tracking delegation metrics helps identify how effectively the NFS server is optimizing file access through delegations and whether adjustments to caching policies or server tuning parameters are necessary. Delegation-related metrics can also reveal potential issues, such as excessive recalls caused by unexpected client contention.

Ultimately, delegations in NFSv4 represent a powerful feature that blends stateful caching with distributed file system principles. By offloading caching responsibilities to clients under controlled conditions, delegations help bridge the performance gap between local and remote file systems while maintaining the data integrity guarantees required in collaborative networked environments. Their successful implementation and management can lead to more efficient NFS deployments that scale effectively and perform reliably across diverse workloads.

NFS Kerberos Authentication

Kerberos authentication within the context of NFS provides a significant enhancement to the security model of this widely-used network file system. Traditional NFS implementations, particularly those relying on NFSv2 and NFSv3, depend on client-side user and group IDs to enforce access control, assuming that both clients and servers share a consistent user identity model. However, this system is vulnerable to spoofing, where a malicious client could impersonate other users simply by manipulating user IDs. To address this weakness, NFSv4 introduced native support for Kerberos, leveraging strong cryptographic authentication to validate users and systems.

Kerberos is a network authentication protocol based on the concept of tickets and symmetric key cryptography. It enables secure mutual authentication between clients and servers within a trusted domain known as a Kerberos realm. The Kerberos authentication system eliminates the need for NFS servers to blindly trust the user identity information presented by clients, instead relying on secure, centralized authentication services to validate identities. This shift transforms NFS from a basic file-sharing tool into a secure and compliant solution suitable for enterprise environments and networks where sensitive data is shared.

Integrating Kerberos with NFS requires that both the NFS server and clients participate in the same Kerberos realm, typically managed by a Key Distribution Center (KDC). The KDC is responsible for issuing tickets that verify the identity of users and services. When a client initiates access to an NFS export secured with Kerberos, it first authenticates with the KDC and obtains a Ticket Granting Ticket (TGT). The client then requests a service ticket specifically for the NFS server. This service ticket is presented during the NFS session establishment, allowing the server to validate the client's credentials cryptographically.

There are three security levels associated with Kerberos authentication in NFS: krb5, krb5i, and krb5p. The krb5 level ensures authentication only, validating the identity of the client and server without modifying the payload of NFS requests and responses. This level is suitable for environments where identity verification is sufficient, and encryption of data in transit is not mandated. The krb5i level adds data integrity checking, ensuring that the data exchanged between client and server is not altered in transit. This protects against man-in-the-middle attacks or data tampering, as each message includes cryptographic checksums verified by both parties. The highest level, krb5p, provides privacy by encrypting all NFS traffic between client and server. This option ensures confidentiality, preventing unauthorized parties from inspecting file data or metadata as it traverses the network.

Setting up Kerberos authentication with NFS requires additional system services, including the rpc.gssd and rpc.svcgssd daemons. The rpc.gssd daemon runs on the client side and is responsible for acquiring and managing Kerberos credentials. It automatically handles the retrieval of Kerberos tickets and provides the necessary tokens for NFS operations. On the server side, the rpc.svcgssd daemon validates incoming Kerberos tickets presented by clients, ensuring that only authenticated and authorized systems can access shared directories.

In addition to system daemons, service principals must be created for the NFS server within the Kerberos realm. A service principal is a unique identity for a network service, formatted as nfs/hostname@REALM. This principal is registered with the KDC and associated with a keytab file that contains the secret keys used to decrypt Kerberos tickets. The NFS server references this keytab file to authenticate client requests securely. Without a valid service principal and keytab, the NFS server cannot participate in Kerberos-authenticated sessions.

When configuring NFS exports with Kerberos security, administrators specify the desired security level using the sec=krb5, sec=krb5i, or sec=krb5p options in the /etc/exports file. For example, an entry such as /srv/securedata 192.168.1.0/24(sec=krb5p,rw,sync) ensures that only clients presenting Kerberos tickets and using encrypted communication can mount and access the directory. On the client side, the corresponding sec option is specified when mounting the NFS share to enforce the same security level.

Kerberos authentication in NFS significantly enhances user-level security by enabling fine-grained access control policies. When integrated with a centralized identity management system such as LDAP or Active Directory, administrators can define access control lists based on authenticated user identities or groups. This allows for granular permission schemes that go beyond traditional UNIX file system permissions. Combined with NFSv4's support for Access Control Lists (ACLs), Kerberos authentication enables complex and highly secure sharing policies that are critical in regulated industries.

Kerberos also facilitates single sign-on (SSO) functionality for NFS clients. Once a user has authenticated and obtained a valid Kerberos ticket, they can access multiple services within the same realm without re-entering their credentials. This simplifies user experience and reduces the risk of password-related vulnerabilities by limiting password transmission across the network.

However, the implementation of Kerberos with NFS is not without challenges. The added complexity requires careful configuration of all participating systems, including correct time synchronization across the network. Kerberos tickets have strict time constraints, and even small discrepancies between client, server, and KDC system clocks can result in authentication failures. Administrators must ensure that all systems use Network Time Protocol (NTP) services to maintain synchronized time.

Additionally, deploying Kerberos-based NFS in environments with mixed operating systems can introduce interoperability considerations. While most modern UNIX-like systems, including Linux and FreeBSD, offer robust Kerberos and NFSv4 support, some legacy systems or non-native NFS implementations may lack full compatibility with Kerberos-secured shares. Testing and validating cross-platform compatibility is an essential step in the deployment process.

Performance is another factor to consider when using Kerberos-secured NFS. The encryption and integrity checks introduced by krb5i and krb5p add computational overhead, which can impact throughput, particularly when handling large files or high I/O workloads. While the overhead is usually acceptable for most environments, performance-sensitive applications may require careful tuning of NFS and Kerberos parameters to balance security and efficiency.

Monitoring Kerberos activity in an NFS deployment is essential to ensure smooth operations and to detect authentication issues. System logs typically contain detailed messages from rpc.gssd and rpc.svcgssd, indicating successful ticket retrieval, service ticket validation, or errors related to authentication failures. Logs from the KDC also provide valuable insight into client and server authentication patterns, aiding in troubleshooting and security audits.

By integrating Kerberos authentication, NFS transitions from a basic file-sharing service reliant on trust-based models to a secure, enterprise-grade solution capable of meeting stringent compliance and regulatory requirements. The combination of centralized authentication, strong cryptographic protection, and NFS's versatile file-sharing capabilities makes this approach highly attractive for organizations prioritizing security and data protection across their networked environments.

NFS and Firewalls

Integrating NFS with firewalls presents unique challenges due to the nature of the protocol and its dependency on multiple services that traditionally operate across dynamically assigned ports. Unlike protocols that use a single well-known port, NFS in versions prior to NFSv4 relies on various daemons and services, such as rpcbind, rpc.mountd, rpc.statd, and nlockmgr, each of which may bind to a random port at runtime. This dynamic port allocation complicates firewall configuration and creates difficulties in environments where strict network segmentation and traffic control are necessary. As firewalls are a critical component of any network security architecture, understanding how to properly configure them for NFS traffic is essential for administrators seeking to balance functionality and security.

In NFSv3 and earlier versions, rpcbind is responsible for mapping RPC program numbers to the ports used by the NFS daemons. When an NFS client initiates communication with a server, it first queries rpcbind to discover which ports are being used for services such as rpc.mountd, nlockmgr, and rpc.statd. Each of these daemons may register on arbitrary ports, forcing administrators to open large port ranges on the firewall to ensure proper functionality. This creates potential vulnerabilities, as broad port openings increase the attack surface of the NFS server, exposing it to unauthorized access attempts or exploitation of vulnerabilities in RPC-based services.

To mitigate this risk, administrators often configure NFS-related daemons to use static ports. By assigning fixed ports to rpc.mountd, rpc.statd, and nlockmgr, it becomes possible to limit firewall openings to only a small set of well-defined ports. For example, the rpc.mountd daemon can be configured to listen on a specific port by modifying its startup options, such as by specifying --port=32767 in the daemon configuration. Similar configurations can be applied to other services to force them to operate on designated ports. This static port assignment provides a more secure firewall posture, allowing administrators to apply precise firewall rules and minimize unnecessary exposure.

In addition to configuring static ports, network administrators must ensure that the firewall allows traffic on the primary NFS service port, TCP and UDP port 2049. This port is used by the nfsd daemon to handle the bulk of NFS file system operations, including file reads, writes, and metadata queries. For environments using NFSv4, this step is significantly simplified, as NFSv4 consolidates all NFS-related operations onto port 2049, reducing the complexity associated with managing multiple daemons and dynamic ports.

When configuring firewalls for NFS traffic, it is essential to consider both the direction and scope of permitted traffic. Generally, firewall rules should allow inbound NFS traffic only from trusted client networks or specific IP addresses, following the principle of least privilege. Allowing unrestricted access to NFS services from the internet or untrusted networks exposes the server to unnecessary risk. Network segmentation strategies, such as isolating NFS servers in dedicated VLANs or zones, further enhance security by reducing the likelihood of unauthorized systems communicating with NFS services.

Stateful inspection is another firewall feature that benefits NFS deployments. Stateful firewalls can track and maintain the state of NFS connections, ensuring that only legitimate traffic associated with established sessions is permitted. This capability is particularly useful for filtering RPC-based services, where multiple ports and short-lived sessions can otherwise lead to difficulties in maintaining effective control over traffic flows.

Administrators should also account for firewall behavior in environments that utilize NFS over TCP compared to UDP. While NFS over UDP was common in older LAN environments due to its low overhead, modern NFS implementations favor TCP for its reliability and improved performance over WANs or networks with higher latency and packet loss. From a firewall perspective, TCP traffic is generally easier to manage, as TCP sessions follow more predictable connection patterns and benefit from TCP's inherent congestion control and retransmission mechanisms.

In highly secure or regulated environments, it may be necessary to implement deep packet inspection (DPI) capabilities in the firewall to analyze and enforce policies based on NFS traffic content. While DPI is more commonly used for application-layer protocols, some next-generation firewalls offer limited inspection capabilities for NFS to detect unusual patterns or anomalous behavior indicative of potential threats, such as unauthorized data exfiltration or NFS-based denial-of-service attempts.

Firewalls deployed in conjunction with NFS should also be configured to log all permitted and denied connection attempts related to NFS services. Log files provide valuable insight into how the firewall is interacting with NFS traffic and can reveal misconfigurations, access attempts from unauthorized clients, or other suspicious activity. Regularly reviewing firewall logs enables administrators to identify and address security concerns proactively.

For organizations operating in cloud or hybrid environments, firewall configuration may extend beyond traditional hardware appliances to include virtualized or software-defined firewalls. Cloud service providers often implement security groups or network security policies that function similarly to firewall rules, controlling ingress and egress traffic based on port and protocol. When deploying NFS servers in cloud environments, administrators must ensure that security group rules are aligned with the server's static port configuration, and that NFS traffic is restricted to known and trusted client IP ranges.

Beyond firewalls, network security best practices for NFS include implementing VPN tunnels or IPsec to encrypt NFS traffic across untrusted or public networks. While NFSv4 with Kerberos sec=krb5p provides encryption at the protocol level, additional transport-layer encryption such as VPNs can add another layer of security, protecting against traffic interception and ensuring confidentiality even if firewall rules are bypassed due to misconfiguration.

Another consideration is the use of fail2ban or similar intrusion prevention systems alongside firewalls to monitor NFS-related logs and automatically block IP addresses that exhibit suspicious behavior, such as repeated failed mount attempts or excessive RPC queries. Automated blocking helps limit exposure to brute-force attacks or scanning activity that may target NFS services.

Administrators should also plan for maintenance and disaster recovery scenarios when configuring firewalls for NFS. For example, during server migrations or failover events in clustered NFS deployments, firewall rules may need to dynamically adjust to allow traffic to newly active nodes. In such cases, integrating firewall configurations with orchestration and automation tools, such as Ansible or Puppet, ensures consistent and reliable rule management.

Properly integrating NFS with firewalls is a multi-faceted task that requires careful planning, from configuring static ports to defining granular access controls and monitoring traffic patterns. The goal is to maintain the functionality of NFS services while minimizing the security risks associated with exposing file-sharing protocols across network boundaries. By combining NFS best practices with sound firewall configurations, organizations can achieve a secure and resilient file-sharing environment suitable for both internal and distributed network architectures.

Automounting NFS Shares

Automounting NFS shares is a technique used to simplify the management of remote file systems in distributed environments. Rather than requiring manual intervention to mount and unmount NFS directories, automounting dynamically mounts remote shares when they are accessed and automatically unmounts them after a period of inactivity. This approach offers several advantages, including improved resource management, reduced administrative overhead, and better integration with user workflows, especially in environments where multiple NFS shares are accessed sporadically by different clients or users.

The primary tool used for automounting NFS shares on most Linux and UNIX systems is the automounter service, commonly implemented through the autofs package. Autofs works by monitoring specific mount points defined in configuration files and triggering mount operations on demand. When a user or application attempts to access a directory configured as an automount point, autofs automatically performs the necessary mount operation to connect to the NFS server and make the remote files available. Once the access is complete and the directory remains idle for a predefined timeout period, autofs automatically unmounts the share, freeing system resources and reducing network load.

The autofs service is typically composed of a master map file and one or more indirect or direct map files. The master map file, usually located at /etc/auto.master, defines the base directories where automounted file systems will appear and specifies the location of the secondary map files containing individual mount configurations. For example, an entry in the master map might define that /mnt/nfs is to be managed by autofs and reference a secondary map file at /etc/auto.nfs. The corresponding /etc/auto.nfs file would then list the specific NFS shares to be automounted within that directory hierarchy.

In indirect maps, the structure defines a directory where multiple automounted subdirectories are created dynamically. For instance, if /mnt/nfs is the base directory, entries in the /etc/auto.nfs file could define subdirectories such as /mnt/nfs/projects or /mnt/nfs/data, each corresponding to a different NFS export. A typical entry might look like projects -rw,soft,intr 192.168.1.10:/srv/nfs/projects, where projects is the directory name under /mnt/nfs, followed by the mount options and the remote NFS path. When a user navigates to /mnt/nfs/projects, autofs automatically mounts the NFS export from the specified server.

Direct maps, on the other hand, allow administrators to define absolute paths that are automounted, bypassing the need for a base directory. Direct maps are typically located at /etc/auto.direct and allow for more granular control over mount points. For example, a direct map entry might look like /projects -rw,soft,intr

192.168.1.10:/srv/nfs/projects, which would cause the /projects directory on the client to be automounted directly from the NFS server.

Automounting provides significant advantages in multi-user environments such as research labs, universities, or enterprise networks where users may only need occasional access to shared directories. Without automounting, administrators would need to maintain static entries in each client's /etc/fstab file, resulting in all NFS shares being mounted at boot time, regardless of whether they are used. This can lead to wasted resources, such as open file handles and unnecessary network traffic, especially when dealing with dozens or hundreds of NFS exports across multiple servers.

Additionally, automounting mitigates certain failure scenarios. If an NFS server is temporarily unavailable, a static mount from /etc/fstab may cause the client system to hang or delay during boot as it waits for the server to respond. With autofs, the system does not attempt to mount the share until it is accessed, and if the server is unreachable at that time, the failure is localized to the user's attempt to access the specific mount point, leaving the rest of the system unaffected.

Autofs also provides configurable timeout settings, typically controlled through the --timeout option in the master map file. For example, setting --timeout=300 causes automounted shares to be unmounted after five minutes of inactivity. This feature helps reduce resource usage and minimizes the impact of idle mounts on the client and server, while still providing transparent access to users when needed.

In terms of mount options, autofs supports the same NFS mount parameters as the traditional mount command, including soft versus hard mounts, timeouts, retransmission counts, and rsize/wsize settings. Administrators can tailor these options based on workload characteristics and network conditions. For example, in environments where network stability is a concern, using hard mounts with TCP transport and increased timeout values may be preferable. In contrast, soft mounts can be used where immediate failure feedback is needed without blocking user processes.

For environments using NFSv4, autofs can be configured to mount shares using the nfs4 file system type, benefiting from NFSv4's enhancements such as stateful locking and integrated ACL support. Automounting NFSv4 shares is no different from NFSv3 from an autofs configuration standpoint, but administrators may wish to specify additional NFSv4-specific options, such as sec=krb5, to enforce Kerberos authentication for secure environments.

Autofs also supports advanced features such as multi-mount maps, where multiple exports can be mounted under a single directory structure. This is particularly useful for aggregating multiple NFS exports into a single namespace, providing users with a consolidated view of distributed file systems. For instance, a /mnt/nfs/home directory could aggregate home directories from several NFS servers by defining multiple subdirectories in a single map file.

Administrators must also consider the impact of automounting on user experience. While automounting is generally seamless, the initial access to an automounted directory may incur a slight delay as autofs initiates the mount process and the client establishes the NFS connection. In most cases, this delay is negligible, but in latency-sensitive environments, optimizing DNS resolution, server response times, and network infrastructure can help minimize any perceptible lag.

Troubleshooting automounting configurations involves checking autofs logs, typically found in /var/log/messages or through journalctl on systemd-based systems. Errors such as map misconfigurations, permission issues, or network timeouts will be recorded here, providing administrators with the necessary information to diagnose and correct issues.

Automounting NFS shares streamlines the process of accessing remote file systems, particularly in dynamic or large-scale environments. By automatically mounting NFS exports only when they are needed and unmounting them when idle, autofs optimizes resource usage while maintaining transparency for end-users. This flexibility, combined with its integration with standard NFS configurations, makes automounting an essential practice for modern NFS deployments in both enterprise and academic settings.

NFS High Availability

Ensuring high availability for NFS is critical in environments where uninterrupted access to shared file systems is essential for business continuity, application stability, and user productivity. High availability in the context of NFS means that shared directories and data must remain accessible even in the event of server failures, network disruptions, or storage outages. Without high availability, any interruption to the NFS server could render critical data inaccessible to clients, leading to application crashes, workflow disruptions, and potential data loss.

One of the most common approaches to achieving high availability with NFS is implementing active-passive failover clusters. In this model, two or more NFS servers are configured so that one server actively handles all NFS requests while the other remains on standby, ready to take over in the event of a failure. These servers are typically connected to a shared storage backend, such as a SAN or NAS, ensuring that the data remains available to either node. Cluster resource management tools like Pacemaker, combined with Corosync for messaging, are frequently used to monitor server health and automate the failover process. When the active NFS server fails, Pacemaker automatically transfers the virtual IP address and the NFS service to the standby node, ensuring that clients can continue accessing data with minimal disruption.

In more complex environments, active-active NFS clusters may be employed, where multiple NFS servers operate simultaneously and serve different parts of the file system or even the same file system using a clustered file system such as GFS2 or OCFS2. This setup provides not only high availability but also load balancing, distributing client requests across multiple servers to improve performance and reduce the risk of bottlenecks. Active-active clustering requires careful planning and advanced configurations to ensure data consistency and integrity, as multiple nodes write to the shared storage simultaneously.

A crucial component of any NFS high availability strategy is the use of reliable and redundant shared storage. High availability cannot be achieved if the storage layer itself is a single point of failure. Shared storage systems should be configured with RAID arrays, redundant controllers, and multiple network paths using multipathing techniques. Multipathing allows storage traffic to continue flowing even if one path fails, providing uninterrupted access to the shared storage. Technologies like iSCSI multipath or Fibre Channel multipath are commonly deployed to achieve this level of redundancy in storage networks.

To enhance NFS availability further, administrators often configure virtual IP addresses that move between NFS servers during failover events. Clients mount the NFS export using the virtual IP, abstracting the physical server from the client's perspective. This ensures that during a failover, clients do not need to remount file systems or change mount configurations, as the virtual IP seamlessly shifts to the standby node. Combining virtual IP addresses with DNS entries that resolve to these IPs adds an additional layer of abstraction, making NFS failover events invisible to end users.

Heartbeat monitoring is a critical component of failover automation. Heartbeat refers to periodic health checks exchanged between nodes in a cluster to confirm that they are operational. If a node fails to send a heartbeat within a specified interval, the cluster manager triggers failover procedures. In the case of NFS, this includes stopping the NFS service on the failed node, starting it on the standby node, migrating the virtual IP, and re-exporting the file systems. The goal is to minimize downtime and automate recovery without requiring manual intervention.

In environments where geographic redundancy is a requirement, NFS high availability can be extended to include disaster recovery (DR) sites. In such configurations, asynchronous or synchronous replication solutions replicate data between primary and secondary data centers. In the event of a catastrophic failure at the primary site, administrators can activate NFS services in the DR site and redirect client traffic accordingly. This approach is essential for organizations that require business continuity during regional outages or natural disasters.

Some enterprises use distributed file systems such as GlusterFS or CephFS in combination with NFS to create highly available and scalable storage backends. These distributed file systems spread data across multiple nodes and storage devices, providing built-in redundancy and resilience to node failures. In GlusterFS, for instance, NFS-Ganesha, a user-space NFS server, can be deployed to serve NFS clients with high availability capabilities backed by Gluster volumes. Such distributed architectures eliminate traditional single points of failure by replicating data across multiple physical nodes.

It is also essential to consider client-side configurations when implementing NFS high availability. Clients should mount NFS shares using options such as hard and intr to handle server failover scenarios gracefully. The hard option ensures that client processes retry NFS requests indefinitely during failover periods, while intr allows users to interrupt stuck processes if needed. Additionally, configuring the automounter (autofs) with failover capabilities enables clients to automatically select the next available server from a list of NFS servers provided in the mount configuration.

Implementing robust monitoring and alerting for NFS servers and clusters is another critical aspect of high availability. Tools such as Nagios, Zabbix, or Prometheus can be configured to monitor NFS service health, cluster status, and storage system performance. Real-time alerts allow administrators to respond to issues proactively before they escalate into full outages. Logging and analyzing NFS traffic and service status can also help identify potential problems and optimize system reliability.

Beyond failover mechanisms, routine testing of high availability configurations is vital to ensure that all components function correctly during real-world failure scenarios. Periodic failover drills, where administrators intentionally simulate node or network failures, validate that the cluster behaves as expected and that services recover within acceptable recovery time objectives (RTOs). Regular testing builds confidence in the system's resilience and helps identify misconfigurations or single points of failure that may have been overlooked.

As cloud adoption grows, some organizations extend NFS high availability into hybrid cloud environments, where on-premises NFS services are integrated with cloud-based file services for additional redundancy and flexibility. Cloud services such as AWS Elastic File System (EFS) or Azure Files offer NFS-compatible storage with built-in availability zones and redundancy, allowing organizations to offload part of their high availability strategy to cloud providers while maintaining familiar NFS interfaces.

By combining failover clusters, distributed storage, network redundancy, and proper client configurations, organizations can build highly available NFS solutions that meet modern business demands for reliability and resilience. Each layer of redundancy and automation contributes to a comprehensive high availability strategy, ensuring that NFS services remain operational even during unexpected failures or planned maintenance activities.

Monitoring NFS Performance

Monitoring NFS performance is essential to ensure that file-sharing services operate efficiently and reliably within an organization's network. Without proper monitoring, performance issues may go undetected until they result in degraded user experience, application slowdowns, or system outages. A comprehensive NFS monitoring strategy involves keeping track of various metrics across both client and server components, identifying bottlenecks, and proactively addressing emerging problems. NFS performance is influenced by factors such as network latency, server workload, disk I/O, and client behavior, all of which must be evaluated regularly to maintain optimal performance.

The nfsstat utility is one of the most valuable tools for monitoring NFS activity. This command-line tool provides statistics on NFS client and server operations, including counts of RPC calls, successful responses, timeouts, retransmissions, and errors. On the server side, nfsstat -s offers insights into how the NFS server is handling incoming requests, breaking them down into read, write, lookup, getattr, and other core file system operations. High levels of retransmissions or timeouts may indicate network issues, insufficient server resources, or improperly tuned client configurations. On the client side, nfsstat -c reveals similar statistics from the perspective of the client, allowing administrators to correlate client behavior with server-side trends.

Another key utility is iostat, which provides information about disk I/O activity on the NFS server. Since NFS performance is closely tied to the speed and responsiveness of the server's underlying storage, monitoring disk read and write rates, I/O wait times, and queue lengths helps determine if the server's storage subsystem is a bottleneck. If iostat reports sustained high utilization or elevated wait times, it may suggest that the server's disks are struggling to keep up with NFS requests, prompting a need for storage optimization or upgrades, such as deploying faster disks or adjusting caching policies.

For network-level monitoring, netstat and ss can provide visibility into active NFS connections, socket statistics, and network errors. These tools help identify whether network congestion, packet drops, or connection limits are contributing to degraded NFS performance. Since NFS traffic often involves sustained high-throughput operations, particularly in data-intensive environments, monitoring network interfaces for saturation or errors is crucial. Complementary tools such as iftop or iptraf can visualize real-time network usage, making it easier to identify clients generating excessive traffic or to detect anomalies indicative of misconfigured systems.

Beyond individual utilities, system-wide performance monitoring frameworks such as sar (from the sysstat package) can collect and report on CPU usage, memory consumption, disk I/O, and network activity over time. Using sar, administrators can establish baseline performance levels and detect deviations that may signal underlying issues. For example, if sar indicates that CPU usage spikes consistently during peak business hours, correlating this data with NFS operation counts may reveal that the server's CPU is overloaded by handling too many concurrent NFS requests.

More advanced environments may implement centralized monitoring systems such as Zabbix, Prometheus, or Nagios. These platforms collect and visualize NFS-related metrics from multiple servers and clients, allowing for real-time dashboards and historical trend analysis. Custom monitoring agents or plugins can be configured to extract specific NFS statistics and alert administrators when predefined thresholds are exceeded. For instance, setting up alerts for excessive NFS server retransmissions, elevated disk I/O wait times, or dropped

NFS mounts can help prevent minor issues from escalating into full-blown outages.

NFS client-side performance monitoring is equally important, as client misconfigurations or suboptimal mount options can negatively impact server load and network performance. Reviewing client mount options such as rsize, wsize, timeo, and retrans helps ensure that clients are using optimal settings for the given network conditions and workloads. Clients operating over WANs or lossy networks may require different tuning parameters compared to those on a local gigabit LAN. Client-side logs, including /var/log/messages or systemd journal logs, can provide additional clues about mounting issues, timeouts, or RPC call failures.

In environments where NFSv4 with delegations is used, administrators should monitor delegation-related metrics. Delegations improve performance by reducing client-server interactions, but excessive delegation recalls due to frequent multi-client access can introduce performance overhead. NFS server logs and nfsstat outputs help track how often delegations are granted, recalled, and returned, providing insight into whether delegations are benefiting or hindering performance based on actual usage patterns.

Monitoring cache efficiency is another important aspect of NFS performance. Both client and server file system caches significantly affect response times and network usage. Metrics related to cache hit rates, especially on the client side, can indicate whether attribute caching and data caching are functioning effectively. Low cache hit rates could point to overly aggressive cache timeout settings or workloads where files are frequently modified across multiple clients, reducing the effectiveness of caching mechanisms.

Additionally, monitoring NFS locking activity can prevent performance degradation caused by lock contention. Excessive or prolonged file locks can cause bottlenecks in multi-client environments, where other clients are forced to wait for locks to be released. Tools such as nfsstat and lockd-specific logs can help identify patterns of lock usage, revealing applications or workflows that may need to be restructured to reduce lock contention.

In high-throughput environments, measuring NFS throughput and latency directly is critical. Tools like nfs-iostat provide detailed statistics about per-mount point read and write performance, helping administrators pinpoint slow mounts or overburdened servers. This granularity aids in determining whether the issue lies with a specific NFS export, client, or underlying network path.

For cloud and hybrid deployments, monitoring should extend to virtual network components, cloud storage backends, and any intermediary layers that could introduce latency or performance bottlenecks. Cloud providers often offer monitoring tools specific to their platforms, such as AWS CloudWatch or Azure Monitor, which can track metrics from NFS-compatible services like EFS or Azure Files. Integrating these metrics with on-premises monitoring solutions creates a unified view of performance across the entire NFS ecosystem.

Ongoing performance monitoring also supports capacity planning and long-term optimization efforts. By analyzing trends in NFS usage, administrators can forecast when storage upgrades, additional servers, or network enhancements will be necessary to accommodate growing demand. Tracking metrics over weeks or months helps identify periods of peak load, common sources of traffic spikes, and areas where system tuning could yield the most benefit.

Ultimately, consistent and proactive monitoring of NFS performance ensures that the system operates within acceptable parameters, reducing the risk of unexpected outages or slowdowns. It enables administrators to make informed decisions based on empirical data, optimizing both NFS configurations and the supporting infrastructure to deliver a stable and responsive file-sharing environment.

NFS in Virtualized Environments

The use of NFS in virtualized environments has become increasingly common as organizations strive to centralize storage, simplify management, and enhance flexibility in their IT infrastructure. Virtualization technologies such as VMware vSphere, KVM, Hyper-V, and others rely heavily on shared storage systems to provide features like live migration, high availability, and disaster recovery. NFS plays a critical role in enabling these capabilities by offering a network-accessible file system that virtual machines (VMs) and hypervisors can use as a storage backend.

One of the primary benefits of using NFS in a virtualized environment is the abstraction it provides between compute and storage layers. By mounting NFS shares on hypervisor hosts, administrators can centralize VM disk images, ISO libraries, templates, and snapshots on a dedicated NFS server or NAS device. This eliminates the need for local storage on each hypervisor, facilitating workload mobility and enabling features such as vMotion in VMware or live migration in KVM. VMs stored on an NFS share can be moved between hypervisors without transferring data across physical disks, allowing seamless transitions with minimal downtime.

NFS is especially attractive in virtualized environments due to its ease of integration and flexibility. Compared to block-level storage protocols like iSCSI or Fibre Channel, NFS operates at the file system level, simplifying configuration and reducing management overhead. Hypervisors can mount NFS shares just like any other networked file system, avoiding the need to present and format individual block devices. This file-level granularity makes it easier to manage and organize VM disk images and related files.

Performance considerations, however, play a significant role when deploying NFS in virtualized environments. NFS is sensitive to network latency and bandwidth, as all VM I/O requests are transmitted over the network to the NFS server. To mitigate performance bottlenecks, it is recommended to use high-speed networking, such as 10 Gigabit Ethernet or faster. Many enterprises also deploy dedicated storage networks or VLANs to isolate NFS traffic from general-purpose data traffic, reducing congestion and ensuring that VM storage traffic receives sufficient bandwidth.

In addition to network performance, the NFS server's hardware must be sized appropriately to handle the I/O demands of multiple hypervisors and VMs. NFS servers should be equipped with fast storage backends, such as SSDs or NVMe devices, configured in RAID arrays to provide redundancy and performance. In environments with high virtual machine density, NFS servers may also implement caching mechanisms or storage acceleration technologies to improve read and write performance. Using server-side caching, whether through dedicated cache disks or integrated memory caching, can significantly reduce the latency experienced by VMs accessing disk images stored on NFS shares.

It is equally important to tune NFS client settings on hypervisors for optimal performance. Mount options such as rsize and wsize, which define the read and write buffer sizes, can be adjusted based on network conditions and workload profiles. Larger buffer sizes generally improve throughput, especially over fast networks, while smaller sizes may reduce latency in certain scenarios. Administrators should also consider setting mount options such as hard and intr to ensure reliable handling of NFS server failover scenarios, preventing hypervisors from hanging indefinitely during storage outages.

NFS in virtualized environments is frequently paired with automation and orchestration platforms, including VMware vCenter, OpenStack, and Kubernetes. In VMware environments, for example, NFS datastores can be registered and managed through vCenter, making it possible to deploy, manage, and migrate VMs using familiar tools. OpenStack environments may use NFS as backend storage for Cinder volumes or Glance image repositories, while Kubernetes can leverage NFS as a persistent volume provider, offering shared storage to containerized applications running on nodes across a cluster.

High availability is a crucial factor when using NFS as a storage backend for virtualization. Any NFS server downtime can disrupt access to VM disks, potentially leading to VM crashes or degraded performance. To address this, NFS servers are often deployed in high-availability clusters using failover solutions such as Pacemaker or in conjunction with distributed file systems like GlusterFS or CephFS. By replicating data across multiple nodes and implementing automatic failover mechanisms, administrators can ensure continuous availability of NFS shares even in the event of server or storage failures.

Snapshot and backup capabilities are additional considerations in NFS-backed virtualized environments. Many NFS servers or NAS appliances offer native snapshot functionality, allowing administrators to create point-in-time copies of VM disk images without disrupting running workloads. Snapshots can be used for quick recovery in case of accidental data loss or corruption. Furthermore, NFS-based storage systems can integrate with backup solutions that support NFS exports, enabling efficient and centralized data protection strategies for all VMs using the shared storage.

Security in NFS configurations for virtualized environments must be carefully managed. Hypervisors mounting NFS shares should do so over secure and controlled networks, preferably isolated from public or untrusted traffic. In addition, administrators should implement export restrictions on the NFS server to limit access to specific hypervisor IP addresses or subnets. For environments requiring higher levels of data protection, NFSv4 with Kerberos authentication and encryption (using sec=krb5p) provides an additional layer of security, ensuring that storage traffic is authenticated and encrypted end-to-end.

Monitoring NFS performance is critical in virtualized environments, as storage bottlenecks can have a cascading impact on VM responsiveness and application performance. Tools such as nfsstat, iostat, and custom monitoring agents integrated with hypervisor platforms can provide visibility into NFS-related metrics, including latency, I/O throughput, and error rates. Regular performance assessments help administrators identify hotspots and make informed decisions regarding capacity planning, storage upgrades, or configuration adjustments.

Some virtualization platforms also allow NFS storage to be used in conjunction with storage policies that define how VMs interact with their storage backends. For example, in VMware environments, administrators can create policies that specify which NFS datastores should be used for certain types of VMs based on performance or redundancy requirements. This allows organizations to segment workloads, ensuring that critical VMs are placed on higher-performing NFS volumes while less demanding workloads use more cost-effective storage.

The growing trend of hybrid cloud adoption has further expanded the use of NFS in virtualized environments. Many public cloud providers offer NFS-compatible file storage services that can be mounted by on-premises or cloud-based hypervisors. This hybrid approach enables organizations to extend their data centers to the cloud, allowing VMs to access centralized NFS shares regardless of their physical location. In such deployments, organizations must consider network latency, secure connectivity, and integration with existing identity and access management systems to maintain consistent performance and security across hybrid infrastructure.

NFS continues to play a pivotal role in supporting virtualized environments due to its simplicity, flexibility, and compatibility with leading virtualization platforms. By following best practices in network design, storage configuration, and security, organizations can leverage NFS to deliver scalable and resilient storage solutions that empower their virtualized workloads to run smoothly and efficiently.

NFS with Containers and Kubernetes

The integration of NFS with containers and Kubernetes has become a common approach to managing persistent storage for applications running in containerized environments. While containers are designed to be lightweight and ephemeral, many real-world applications require persistent storage to retain data across container restarts, failures, or migrations. NFS, with its ability to provide centralized, network-accessible file systems, offers an effective solution to meet these storage requirements in Kubernetes clusters and container ecosystems.

In Kubernetes, applications run inside pods, which can be scheduled across any node in the cluster. Since local storage on a node is temporary and tied to the node's lifecycle, Kubernetes needs external storage systems to provide data persistence beyond the pod or node lifespan. NFS serves as a networked file system that allows pods on different nodes to access a shared file system, ensuring that data remains available even if a pod is rescheduled to a different node due to scaling, updates, or failures.

A common use case for NFS in Kubernetes is to create persistent volumes (PVs) backed by NFS exports. Persistent volumes are abstractions within Kubernetes that represent external storage resources. Administrators can configure PVs that point to directories exported from an NFS server, making those directories available to pods via persistent volume claims (PVCs). PVCs are requests for storage by applications, and Kubernetes automatically binds them to available PVs. This mechanism decouples storage provisioning from application deployment, simplifying the developer experience while ensuring that the underlying storage is handled consistently.

Configuring an NFS-backed persistent volume in Kubernetes typically involves defining a YAML manifest specifying details such as the NFS server IP, the path of the export, and access modes like ReadWriteMany (RWX), which allows multiple pods to read and write simultaneously. The RWX mode is one of the key advantages of using NFS, as it supports concurrent access to the same data from multiple pods, making it ideal for shared workloads such as content management systems, shared file repositories, or collaborative applications that require multiple application instances to work on the same set of files.

NFS can also be integrated with Kubernetes through dynamic provisioning using external storage provisioners. A storage provisioner automates the creation of persistent volumes when a PVC is submitted, reducing the need for manual intervention. For NFS, dynamic provisioners like the nfs-client-provisioner act as intermediaries that automatically create subdirectories in a specified NFS export and bind them to PVCs as unique persistent volumes. This approach streamlines storage management and enables Kubernetes to handle persistent storage in a more cloud-native manner.

When deploying NFS within a Kubernetes cluster, performance and security considerations must be taken into account. From a performance perspective, since NFS relies on network connectivity, it is important to deploy NFS servers on high-speed networks, preferably with dedicated storage backends optimized for container workloads. Latency and throughput can affect application responsiveness, especially when multiple pods are accessing the same NFS share concurrently. Administrators may need to tune mount options such as rsize, wsize, and caching behaviors on Kubernetes nodes to ensure optimal performance.

Security is another important aspect of using NFS in Kubernetes. By default, NFS relies on client-side user and group IDs for access control, which may be insufficient for multi-tenant or security-sensitive environments. To mitigate risks, NFS exports should be restricted to specific IP ranges or Kubernetes node subnets to prevent unauthorized access. In addition, running NFSv4 with Kerberos authentication enhances security by enforcing cryptographic identity verification and optionally encrypting traffic between Kubernetes nodes and the NFS server.

For Kubernetes workloads requiring higher levels of data protection, administrators may also use network policies and firewall rules to limit NFS traffic to only authorized pods and namespaces. Combining Kubernetes-native security features like role-based access control (RBAC) with external NFS access restrictions helps enforce a multi-layered security model.

In containerized environments outside of Kubernetes, such as Docker standalone setups, NFS can also be used to mount shared directories into running containers. Docker supports mounting NFS shares as volumes by specifying the NFS server address and export path in the volume configuration. This enables containers to access the same shared storage regardless of the host machine they are running on, facilitating scenarios like shared caches, distributed build directories, or common log repositories.

NFS with containers also enables stateful applications to run more effectively. Applications like databases, file servers, or analytics tools often require persistent storage to function correctly. By integrating NFS as the storage backend, these applications can retain their data across container lifecycle events and across different nodes in distributed setups. It is important, however, to carefully evaluate whether NFS is suitable for latency-sensitive or high-I/O applications, as its network-based nature may introduce performance constraints compared to local or block-level storage.

With the rise of microservices architectures in Kubernetes, NFS has become a key tool for scenarios where microservices need shared access to common files. For example, a set of stateless web servers running in separate pods may need to serve static assets such as images, videos, or configuration files. Instead of bundling these assets with each container image or synchronizing them manually, administrators can mount a shared NFS volume to all relevant pods, ensuring consistent access to updated files.

As Kubernetes environments grow in scale, monitoring the performance and availability of NFS shares becomes increasingly important. Monitoring tools such as Prometheus with custom exporters or plugins can collect metrics on NFS operations, latency, throughput, and error rates. These metrics help administrators identify bottlenecks, capacity constraints, or issues with NFS server availability that may affect the Kubernetes workloads relying on the shared storage.

For high availability in production-grade environments, NFS servers used in Kubernetes clusters should be part of a highly available storage setup. This may involve deploying NFS servers in active-passive failover clusters or using distributed file systems like GlusterFS or CephFS with NFS-Ganesha as a frontend. Such architectures ensure that Kubernetes workloads can continue to access persistent storage even if a node or storage device fails, providing greater resilience to infrastructure outages.

Ultimately, integrating NFS with containers and Kubernetes offers a reliable and flexible way to deliver persistent shared storage in dynamic and distributed environments. Whether through static PVs, dynamic provisioning, or container-level NFS mounts, the use of NFS simplifies storage management while enabling advanced application use cases that require data persistence and shared access. By combining NFS with Kubernetes' powerful orchestration capabilities, organizations can support modern, containerized applications with efficient and centralized storage infrastructure.

Common NFS Errors and Troubleshooting

Despite its reliability and wide adoption, NFS can encounter various issues in day-to-day operations, especially when deployed in complex or high-demand environments. Understanding common NFS errors and the appropriate troubleshooting techniques is crucial for administrators who manage file-sharing infrastructures. Many problems stem from misconfigurations, network issues, permission mismatches, or software bugs, but with systematic diagnosis, most NFS errors can be resolved effectively.

One of the most common errors in NFS environments is the stale NFS file handle error. This occurs when a client tries to access a file or directory on an NFS-mounted share, but the object has been deleted or moved on the server since the client cached the file handle. The file handle, which the client uses to locate the file on the server, is no longer valid, leading to an error message such as stale NFS file handle or Input/output error. To resolve this, administrators typically force the client to remount the affected NFS share, clearing the outdated file handle cache. In environments where files are frequently modified or moved, reducing attribute caching durations on the client can help mitigate the frequency of stale handle errors.

Another common issue is mount failures, often indicated by messages like mount.nfs: access denied by server or mount.nfs: requested NFS version or transport protocol is not supported. These errors usually point to mismatches between client mount options and server export settings. For example, if a server is configured to export a directory using NFSv4 but a client attempts to mount it using NFSv3, the mount will fail. Similarly, if the client's IP address or hostname does not match the access control lists defined in the server's /etc/exports file, the server will reject the mount request. Troubleshooting this requires verifying the client's mount command or /etc/fstab entry, ensuring the correct NFS version and options are used, and checking the server's export configuration for any discrepancies.

Permissions and ownership issues are another frequent challenge when working with NFS. Because NFS relies on numeric user and group IDs to enforce permissions, mismatched ID mappings between the client and server can result in denied access or unexpected behavior, such as files appearing to be owned by the nobody user. These issues are common in environments where user and group databases are not synchronized. A common resolution involves implementing centralized identity management systems like LDAP or NIS to ensure consistent UID and GID values across all NFS clients and servers.

Alternatively, administrators can use export options such as all_squash combined with anonuid and anongid settings to remap all client requests to a specific user on the server.

Performance-related errors can manifest as slow NFS mounts, delayed file operations, or high application latency. These symptoms often point to network congestion, high server CPU or disk I/O utilization, or suboptimal mount options. Using tools such as nfsstat, iostat, and netstat can help identify whether the bottleneck is occurring on the network, server, or client. For example, high retransmission rates or frequent timeout errors in nfsstat output suggest network instability or excessive latency. Adjusting mount options such as timeo and retrans, upgrading to TCP transport instead of UDP, or segmenting NFS traffic onto a dedicated storage network are common solutions.

Locking problems, particularly in NFSv3 environments, can cause applications to hang or fail unexpectedly. These problems are typically linked to the Network Lock Manager (NLM) or rpc.statd daemons, which are responsible for managing file locks in stateless NFS versions. If these services are not running properly on either the client or server, file locking may fail, preventing applications from accessing locked files or causing data corruption. In NFSv4, integrated locking mechanisms reduce the likelihood of such issues, but lock contention between clients accessing the same files can still degrade performance or cause application stalls. Monitoring lock usage and considering file-level or application-level changes to reduce lock contention are important troubleshooting steps.

Firewall misconfigurations can also interfere with NFS operations. In NFSv3, where auxiliary daemons such as rpc.mountd and rpc.lockd may use dynamic ports, improper firewall settings can prevent clients from establishing necessary connections, resulting in mount failures or timeouts. Ensuring that the firewall allows traffic on all required NFS and RPC-related ports, or configuring static ports for these services, is a best practice. NFSv4 simplifies firewall configurations by consolidating operations onto port 2049, but it still requires attention to firewall rules to ensure proper access between clients and servers.

Authentication errors may arise in environments using NFSv4 with Kerberos security. Messages such as Permission denied or gssd: can't acquire credentials indicate problems with Kerberos ticket acquisition or configuration. These issues can result from expired or missing Kerberos tickets on the client, incorrect service principal configurations on the server, or clock skew between client, server, and KDC systems. Ensuring that all systems are time-synchronized using NTP, validating keytab entries, and confirming that rpc.gssd and rpc.svcgssd services are running can help resolve authentication-related errors.

Unmounting issues occasionally occur, particularly in the presence of stale NFS mounts. If an NFS server becomes unavailable or unresponsive, clients may hang when attempting to unmount the NFS share. Using the lazy unmount option (umount -l) can help detach the mount point without waiting for the server to respond, allowing administrators to proceed with troubleshooting or server recovery. Additionally, automounter services like autofs can be configured to manage mount and unmount operations automatically, reducing the likelihood of user-facing unmount errors.

In clustered environments or deployments using high availability configurations, split-brain conditions or network partitions may cause clients to mount different servers exporting the same NFS share, leading to data inconsistency or corruption. These issues require careful cluster configuration to ensure that only one node exports a given share at any time, often enforced through cluster resource management tools like Pacemaker.

When dealing with persistent or complex NFS errors, enabling verbose logging on the server and client can provide valuable insights. Increasing the log level for NFS daemons or kernel modules allows administrators to capture detailed diagnostic messages that can reveal subtle configuration issues or underlying system problems. For example, kernel logs may show permission denials related to SELinux or AppArmor profiles that block certain NFS operations, requiring policy adjustments to restore functionality.

Troubleshooting NFS involves a multi-layered approach, examining client configurations, server settings, network infrastructure, and application behavior. By systematically analyzing logs, monitoring tools, and configuration files, administrators can resolve common NFS errors and optimize the file-sharing environment to ensure stable and high-performing services across the network.

NFS Exports in Multi-User Environments

Managing NFS exports in multi-user environments requires a careful balance between accessibility, performance, and security. In such environments, multiple clients, often running on different systems, need to access shared file systems on a central NFS server. Each user or group of users may have unique permission requirements, workflows, and usage patterns that must be accommodated. The complexity of managing NFS exports grows as the number of users and the variety of access needs increase, making it critical to design a robust export strategy that meets operational demands while protecting sensitive data.

At the core of NFS exports in multi-user settings is the /etc/exports file, where administrators define which directories are shared and which clients or networks are permitted to access them. In a multi-user environment, this file often contains multiple entries, each specifying different access control rules tailored to individual teams, departments, or applications. Export entries can include client-specific options that define whether access is read-only or read-write, as well as how user permissions and root privileges are handled on the client side.

One of the most important options when configuring exports for multiple users is root_squash. This option ensures that the root user on a client machine is mapped to an anonymous user on the server, typically the nfsnobody user. This prevents clients' root users from bypassing file system permissions and gaining unrestricted access to files on the server. In multi-user environments where different organizations or departments share the same NFS server, enabling root_squash on all exports is a best practice for mitigating privilege escalation risks.

In some situations, however, certain trusted clients or specific use cases may require full root access to the NFS share. In these cases, administrators may selectively apply the no_root_squash option for those clients only, while maintaining root_squash for all others. Careful application of this setting is necessary to avoid security vulnerabilities, and such decisions should be supported by strong network-level restrictions and identity verification measures to ensure that only authorized systems can connect with elevated privileges.

Export options like all_squash and anonuid/anongid provide additional control over how user permissions are managed. The all_squash option maps all user requests from the client to the anonymous user on the server, regardless of the client's user or group IDs. This can be useful when exporting public or shared directories where fine-grained user-level permissions are not needed, and administrators prefer to enforce broad access policies. Combining all_squash with a specific anonuid and anongid ensures that all file operations are performed under a dedicated user identity, simplifying file ownership and permission management on the server.

File and directory permissions must be carefully coordinated between the server and clients to ensure proper access control. NFS relies on the consistency of user and group IDs across all connected systems. In environments without centralized identity management, mismatched UIDs and GIDs can cause users to lose access to files or inadvertently inherit elevated privileges. To mitigate this, many organizations deploy directory services such as LDAP or Active Directory to synchronize identity information across all NFS clients and the server. This ensures that when a user on one client creates or modifies a file, the correct ownership and permissions are recognized consistently across the environment.

In more complex scenarios, administrators may use NFSv4's support for Access Control Lists (ACLs) to fine-tune file-level permissions beyond the traditional owner-group-other model. ACLs allow specific permissions to be granted to individual users or groups, supporting more granular access control in shared environments. For example, administrators can permit read-only access to a specific directory for one group while granting full read-write permissions to another group within the same export. ACLs are particularly useful when different teams or departments collaborate on shared datasets but require different levels of access to certain files.

Network segmentation and export isolation further enhance security in multi-user environments. By defining exports with specific client subnet restrictions, administrators can limit access to sensitive data based on physical or logical network boundaries. For example, an export intended for a finance department could be limited to clients within a specific VLAN or IP subnet, preventing access from users outside of that segment. Combining these restrictions with host-based firewalls on the NFS server further hardens the environment against unauthorized access attempts.

Performance considerations also come into play when managing NFS exports for large user bases. In environments with many simultaneous users, read and write workloads can place significant demands on the server's resources. To optimize performance, administrators may implement export-specific tuning options such as async, which allows the server to acknowledge write requests before committing data to disk, improving responsiveness at the expense of some data durability. While async can enhance throughput in certain use cases, it is essential to evaluate the trade-offs based on the criticality of the data.

Some organizations choose to distribute exports across multiple NFS servers to balance the load and minimize bottlenecks. For example, one server may handle exports for development teams, while another manages exports for production workloads. This distribution strategy reduces contention for server resources and allows for export configurations that are tailored to each team's specific performance and security requirements.

Automounting is often used in multi-user NFS environments to simplify client-side management of shared directories. Using autofs, administrators can configure client systems to mount NFS shares automatically when users access specific directories, reducing the need for static mounts in /etc/fstab files and improving system boot times. Automounting is particularly helpful when users only require periodic access to certain exports, as it reduces the overhead of maintaining always-on mounts and ensures that mounts are available on demand.

To maintain visibility and accountability in multi-user NFS deployments, logging and auditing are critical. Server logs, including exportfs and system log files, provide insights into mount attempts, access patterns, and potential misconfigurations. More advanced auditing solutions can track file-level operations, helping organizations meet compliance requirements and detect unauthorized or suspicious activity within shared exports.

Managing NFS exports in multi-user environments demands a comprehensive approach that balances flexibility, performance, and security. Administrators must navigate a complex landscape of user access needs, export configurations, identity management, and network security to create a cohesive and reliable file-sharing infrastructure. By leveraging NFS's export capabilities alongside complementary technologies such as ACLs, automounting, and centralized identity services, organizations can deliver shared storage solutions that meet the diverse needs of multiple user groups while maintaining strict control over data access and system resources.

Using NFS for Backup and Archiving

Network File System (NFS) has been a fundamental technology in networked environments for decades, offering an efficient way to share and access files across different machines as if they were local. When it comes to backup and archiving strategies, NFS plays a critical role in simplifying workflows, increasing flexibility, and reducing costs. Organizations that operate distributed systems or need centralized storage often turn to NFS as a reliable and proven solution for their data protection needs. Understanding how NFS works in the context of backup and archiving is essential for IT administrators and system architects looking to implement resilient and scalable infrastructure.

NFS allows a client machine to mount a remote file system located on an NFS server and interact with it as though it were part of the local file hierarchy. This transparency makes it an ideal candidate for backup operations where remote storage must be treated like local disks. Backup processes that utilize NFS benefit from ease of access and consistent file system semantics, especially in Unix-like environments. Applications and scripts that handle backups can seamlessly write data to NFS-mounted directories without significant modification, simplifying automation and integration into existing backup pipelines.

One of the key advantages of using NFS for backup is its compatibility with a wide range of backup tools and software suites. Popular backup solutions such as rsync, Bacula, Amanda, and commercial enterprise-grade software often support NFS out of the box. This allows IT teams to design backup strategies that leverage NFS shares as backup targets, where snapshots, incremental backups, and full archives can be stored and managed. By centralizing backup data on an NFS server, organizations can ensure that backups from multiple machines or nodes are consolidated, streamlining administration and improving visibility over backup assets.

NFS also offers significant benefits for archiving purposes. Long-term data archiving is crucial for regulatory compliance, historical record-keeping, and disaster recovery planning. With NFS, archived data can be stored on dedicated storage systems that are configured with large-capacity disks or even connected to tape libraries via hierarchical storage management solutions. The flexibility of NFS enables archived datasets to be accessed when needed while remaining in a separate location from production environments, reducing the risk of data loss due to accidental deletion or system failures.

Another important consideration is scalability. As the volume of data that organizations generate continues to grow, NFS provides a scalable framework that allows storage to expand with demand. Administrators can add additional disks or nodes to the NFS server infrastructure, creating more capacity for backups and archives without disrupting existing operations. Moreover, since NFS operates over standard TCP/IP networks, organizations can leverage existing network infrastructure without needing to invest in proprietary or specialized hardware, further reducing operational expenses.

Security is a common concern when using NFS for backup and archiving, especially when sensitive or critical data is involved. Modern implementations of NFS, such as NFSv4, address many of these concerns by incorporating strong authentication and access control mechanisms. Integration with Kerberos for secure authentication and the ability to enforce access control lists (ACLs) on shared filesystems enhance the security posture of NFS deployments. IT teams should follow best practices, including isolating NFS traffic on dedicated network segments or using VPNs to encrypt data in transit, to further mitigate risks associated with data interception or unauthorized access.

Performance is another factor that influences the choice of NFS in backup and archiving scenarios. NFS servers can be optimized to deliver high throughput and low latency by tuning export options, adjusting network parameters, and deploying fast storage media such as solid-state drives (SSDs). Combining NFS with advanced file system features such as ZFS or Btrfs on the server side can also improve performance and provide additional benefits, such as snapshot capabilities, checksumming, and data deduplication. These features contribute to the overall efficiency and reliability of backup and archival processes.

For environments with virtualized workloads or containerized applications, NFS continues to offer advantages. Many hypervisors and container orchestration platforms support NFS as a shared storage backend. This makes it easy to centralize and automate backup tasks in dynamic environments where workloads frequently move between hosts or scale up and down according to demand. By exporting NFS shares to virtual machines or containers, administrators can ensure that data is persistently available for backup operations regardless of where the workload resides within the infrastructure.

Additionally, NFS simplifies disaster recovery workflows by enabling remote replication and off-site backup capabilities. An NFS share can be mounted by backup servers in different geographical locations, allowing for the creation of redundant copies of critical data in case of catastrophic failures or natural disasters. When combined with backup software that supports replication or remote sync, NFS helps organizations achieve greater resilience and meet stringent recovery point objectives (RPOs) and recovery time objectives (RTOs).

Finally, the simplicity and transparency of NFS make it particularly attractive for small to medium-sized businesses that may not have the resources to deploy more complex storage area networks (SANs) or object storage systems. NFS provides a well-understood, easy-to-manage alternative that delivers dependable performance and interoperability across heterogeneous systems. Whether it is for short-term backups, long-term archives, or hybrid solutions combining both,

NFS remains a cornerstone in data protection strategies across a wide variety of industries and use cases. Its maturity, coupled with continued improvements in security and performance, ensures that NFS will remain relevant in modern IT ecosystems where data availability and durability are paramount.

Cross-Platform NFS Sharing

Cross-platform NFS sharing has become a critical capability for modern IT environments that operate with a diverse array of operating systems and hardware platforms. The ability to seamlessly share files between Linux, Unix, macOS, and even Windows systems using Network File System (NFS) provides organizations with the flexibility and interoperability necessary to support a variety of workflows and applications. As enterprises increasingly adopt hybrid infrastructures combining legacy systems with modern cloud-native technologies, the importance of robust cross-platform file sharing mechanisms like NFS continues to grow.

At its core, NFS was originally designed for Unix-based systems, providing a standardized method for sharing files over a network so that remote directories could be mounted and accessed as though they were local. Over time, NFS has evolved to become a widely adopted protocol supported across multiple platforms. This evolution has made NFS an indispensable tool in heterogeneous environments where systems running different operating systems need to exchange data efficiently. Today, NFS sharing is common not only in traditional datacenters but also in cloud environments, research facilities, and even small business networks where cross-platform compatibility is essential.

One of the primary advantages of NFS in cross-platform scenarios is its simplicity. The NFS server can be configured to export directories that can then be mounted by client systems running different operating systems. For example, a Linux server could export a shared directory that is mounted by both a macOS workstation and a Unix server, allowing all systems to read and write files to the same location. This capability is invaluable in mixed-OS environments where teams may use different tools and platforms but still require access to a common set of files.

NFSv3 and NFSv4 are the most commonly used versions in cross-platform setups. NFSv3 offers excellent compatibility and is widely supported, while NFSv4 introduces enhanced features such as stronger security through Kerberos authentication, better performance tuning, and support for ACLs. While NFSv4 is often the preferred choice for more secure and complex environments, NFSv3 still finds extensive use, particularly where older operating systems or embedded devices are present. Cross-platform compatibility often hinges on understanding which version of NFS each client can support and configuring the NFS server to accommodate these differences.

When sharing files across different platforms using NFS, administrators often encounter challenges related to file permissions and ownership. This is largely because Unix-like systems, such as Linux and macOS, rely on user IDs (UIDs) and group IDs (GIDs) to determine access rights, while Windows uses a different security model based on Security Identifiers (SIDs) and Access Control Lists (ACLs). To address this disparity, administrators may need to map UIDs and GIDs across systems or leverage features like NFSv4 ACLs that provide a more granular and flexible permission model compatible with multiple operating systems. Proper planning and implementation of UID/GID mapping can prevent common issues, such as users on one system being unable to access files created on another due to mismatched IDs.

Performance optimization is another important consideration when implementing cross-platform NFS sharing. Factors such as network latency, file system differences, and NFS version mismatches can all affect performance. Administrators often need to fine-tune NFS mount options and server export settings to ensure efficient file transfers and access times. For instance, adjusting read and write buffer sizes or enabling asynchronous writes can significantly improve throughput, especially when transferring large files or operating over wide area networks. Similarly, enabling features like attribute caching on the client side can reduce redundant network calls and enhance responsiveness.

Security in cross-platform NFS environments requires careful attention. Since NFS was originally designed for trusted internal networks, it historically lacked strong security mechanisms. However, modern implementations, especially with NFSv4, offer improvements through encryption and authentication features. Organizations should consider deploying NFS over secure VPN tunnels or isolating NFS traffic on dedicated VLANs to minimize exposure. Additionally, using Kerberos-based authentication with NFSv4 helps enforce stronger user identity verification across systems with differing security models, such as integrating Linux systems with an Active Directory domain for Windows compatibility.

Integration with Windows systems has historically posed specific challenges when using NFS. Although Windows is not a native NFS client, Microsoft provides NFS client and server services as part of its Windows Services for UNIX and later through Windows Subsystem for Linux (WSL) and NFS features in Windows Server editions. This allows Windows machines to mount and interact with NFS shares hosted by Unix-like systems, albeit with some limitations. For example, certain Windows applications might not fully support Unix-style file permissions, leading to inconsistencies in how files are handled. Despite these limitations, cross-platform teams can still achieve effective file sharing with NFS, particularly when combined with appropriate configuration and compatibility adjustments.

The rise of virtualization and containerization technologies has further highlighted the importance of cross-platform NFS sharing. In cloud-native environments, it is common to find Linux-based containers running alongside virtual machines that may use Windows or other operating systems. NFS provides a simple and efficient mechanism for sharing persistent storage across these different workloads. Kubernetes, for instance, supports NFS as a persistent volume backend, enabling containerized applications to access shared storage managed by NFS servers. Similarly, virtual machine platforms such as VMware and Hyper-V can leverage NFS datastores for VM storage, enabling file sharing between VMs and physical servers regardless of their operating systems.

Cross-platform NFS sharing also plays a pivotal role in collaborative workflows. In development environments where teams use a mix of macOS, Linux, and Windows machines, NFS allows all users to work on the same codebase, access shared datasets, and manage project files without having to constantly transfer data between systems. This accelerates development cycles and reduces errors related to version control or file synchronization. By providing a common storage platform accessible from any system, NFS fosters improved productivity and more streamlined collaboration among teams with diverse hardware and software preferences.

Despite its benefits, administrators must regularly monitor and maintain NFS environments to ensure long-term reliability and performance. Regularly auditing access controls, updating NFS server software, and reviewing network configurations are essential practices. By proactively addressing compatibility issues and security risks, organizations can continue to leverage NFS as a dependable and efficient solution for cross-platform file sharing well into the future. As new operating systems and technologies emerge, NFS's openness and adaptability will remain key factors in its ability to bridge gaps between disparate systems, enabling seamless data exchange in complex and evolving IT landscapes.

NFS and Storage Area Networks

The relationship between Network File System (NFS) and Storage Area Networks (SANs) represents a convergence of two essential technologies in modern data center and enterprise IT environments. Both NFS and SANs serve critical roles in enabling efficient data storage, access, and management, but they operate at different layers of the infrastructure stack. Understanding how these technologies can complement each other is key to designing highly available, scalable, and high-performance storage solutions for organizations of all sizes.

NFS is a protocol that allows client machines to mount remote file systems over a network, making remote directories appear as if they are part of the local file system hierarchy. It operates over standard IP-based networks, providing file-level access to shared storage resources. On the other hand, SANs operate at the block level, providing raw storage volumes to servers over specialized networking technologies such as Fibre Channel or iSCSI. Unlike NFS, which enables access to files and directories, SANs present block devices that servers format and manage as they would with a local disk.

When combined, NFS and SANs deliver complementary capabilities. A common architecture involves running NFS servers on hosts that connect to storage provided by a SAN. In this setup, the SAN provides high-performance, low-latency block storage to the NFS server, which in turn exports file systems to client machines over IP networks using NFS. This model is widely adopted in environments where multiple servers, virtual machines, or even containers need concurrent access to the same shared storage without each system requiring direct SAN access.

One of the key benefits of this architecture is that it abstracts complex SAN configurations from client systems. End users and applications interacting with NFS shares do not need to be aware of the underlying block storage or Fibre Channel fabrics used by the SAN. Instead, they access familiar file and directory structures over a standard IP network, greatly simplifying deployment and management. This model also reduces costs by limiting the number of systems that require expensive SAN host bus adapters (HBAs) or specialized SAN configurations, centralizing this responsibility on the NFS servers.

Another advantage of integrating NFS with SANs is the ability to leverage the performance and reliability benefits of SAN hardware while maintaining the simplicity and flexibility of NFS at the client level. SANs are known for their high throughput and low latency, characteristics that are critical in environments with heavy storage demands, such as database clusters, virtualization hosts, and enterprise applications. By using a SAN as backend storage for NFS servers, organizations can ensure that file-level access over NFS inherits these performance characteristics, delivering faster file access and improved application responsiveness.

High availability is another important factor in NFS and SAN integration. Most enterprise SANs offer robust features such as multipathing, failover capabilities, and redundancy at the hardware level. These features contribute to minimizing downtime and ensuring continuous access to critical data. When NFS servers are deployed on top of a SAN, administrators can implement clustering solutions or active-passive failover configurations for the NFS servers themselves, further enhancing the resiliency of the storage infrastructure. In such configurations, if one NFS server fails, another node can take over, ensuring uninterrupted access to NFS shares by client systems.

This layered approach also supports scalability. As organizations grow and data volumes increase, SANs can scale by adding additional storage arrays or expanding existing ones. Since the NFS servers interface directly with the SAN, expanding the backend storage pool does not require reconfiguration on the NFS clients. New storage volumes can be provisioned on the SAN, formatted and mounted on the NFS server, and then exported as additional NFS shares to client machines. This elasticity allows organizations to respond quickly to changing storage needs without significant disruptions.

From an administrative perspective, combining NFS with SANs can streamline storage management. SANs often include advanced features such as thin provisioning, snapshots, replication, and data deduplication, which can be leveraged by the NFS servers to enhance storage efficiency and data protection. For example, a snapshot of a SAN-provided volume can serve as a backup for the file system exported via NFS, enabling rapid recovery in case of accidental data loss or corruption. Similarly, SAN-based replication technologies can be used to replicate NFS-exported file systems to remote locations for disaster recovery purposes.

However, this integration is not without challenges. One consideration is the potential for performance bottlenecks at the NFS server level, particularly in environments with many clients or high I/O workloads. Since all client requests must pass through the NFS server to access data stored on the SAN, the NFS server can become a chokepoint if not properly sized. To mitigate this risk, administrators may deploy multiple NFS servers in load-balanced or clustered configurations, distribute file systems across different servers, or leverage parallel NFS (pNFS) to spread workloads more evenly across multiple storage nodes.

Security is another aspect that must be carefully addressed. While SANs typically operate within secure, isolated environments, NFS shares are often accessible over broader IP networks, increasing the potential attack surface. Organizations should implement best practices such as restricting NFS exports to specific IP addresses, using NFSv4 with Kerberos authentication, and isolating NFS traffic on dedicated VLANs. Additionally, proper access control mechanisms must be in place to ensure that users and applications accessing NFS shares only have the permissions necessary for their roles.

In virtualized environments, this combination of NFS and SANs is particularly common. Hypervisors like VMware vSphere and Microsoft Hyper-V frequently use SAN storage for virtual machine (VM) disks, while also relying on NFS datastores for shared file storage, templates, and ISOs. In Kubernetes and other container orchestration platforms, NFS shares backed by SAN storage can provide persistent storage to containers, enabling stateful workloads to run in dynamic, cloud-native environments with enterprise-grade storage capabilities.

Ultimately, the integration of NFS and SANs provides organizations with a versatile and powerful storage solution that blends the best of both file-level and block-level access methods. It enables centralized storage management, high performance, and seamless scalability while supporting a wide range of use cases from traditional enterprise applications to modern cloud-native deployments. By leveraging the strengths of both technologies, IT teams can build resilient storage architectures capable of meeting the evolving demands of today's complex and fast-paced business environments.

NFS and Cloud Integrations

The integration of Network File System (NFS) with cloud platforms has become increasingly important as organizations transition from traditional on-premises infrastructure to hybrid and fully cloud-based architectures. NFS, long established as a robust and widely-used protocol for file sharing in local networks, is now playing a significant role in facilitating seamless storage access within cloud environments. Its simplicity, flexibility, and compatibility with various operating systems and applications make NFS a practical choice for businesses seeking to leverage the scalability and agility of the cloud while maintaining familiar storage workflows.

As more enterprises adopt cloud solutions, one of the challenges they face is ensuring that applications and users can access shared storage resources across distributed environments. NFS addresses this challenge by providing a consistent method for sharing file systems between on-premises systems and cloud-based workloads. Many public cloud providers, including Amazon Web Services (AWS), Microsoft Azure, and Google Cloud Platform (GCP), now offer NFS-compatible services, allowing organizations to mount NFS shares directly within their cloud instances or virtual machines. This compatibility ensures that applications relying on NFS can transition smoothly to cloud environments without the need for significant re-engineering or changes in data access patterns.

One of the most common cloud services offering NFS support is Amazon Elastic File System (EFS). EFS is a fully managed NFS file system designed to be highly available and scalable, providing elastic storage that automatically grows and shrinks based on usage. Cloud-based applications running on Amazon EC2 instances or container services like Amazon ECS and EKS can mount EFS file systems over the NFSv4 protocol, accessing data with the same semantics and structure as they would on traditional on-premises NFS servers. This simplifies migration efforts and enables hybrid cloud models where applications can run across both cloud and on-premises infrastructure while accessing the same data repositories.

Microsoft Azure also provides NFS-compatible file storage through Azure NetApp Files and Azure Files with NFS support. These services allow organizations to provision file shares accessible via NFSv3 or NFSv4.1, making them suitable for enterprise workloads that require low-latency access to shared files. Similarly, Google Cloud Filestore provides fully managed NFS file systems that integrate natively with Google Compute Engine and Kubernetes Engine, offering persistent storage for cloud-based virtual machines and containers. These managed services reduce the operational burden on IT teams, as cloud providers handle much of the complexity related to scalability, availability, and maintenance.

The integration of NFS with cloud environments extends beyond basic file sharing. NFS also plays a pivotal role in supporting modern DevOps workflows, data analytics pipelines, and cloud-native applications. In DevOps practices, continuous integration and continuous deployment (CI/CD) systems often require access to shared file storage for storing build artifacts, configuration files, and logs. By utilizing NFS shares in the cloud, teams can maintain centralized storage repositories that are accessible from multiple build agents and deployment environments, improving collaboration and streamlining automation processes.

In big data and analytics use cases, NFS serves as a backend for storing large datasets that need to be processed by distributed computing frameworks such as Apache Hadoop, Spark, or cloud-native analytics services. Mounting an NFS share as a common data source for these platforms enables analysts and data engineers to access, transform, and analyze data without duplicating it across multiple storage locations. This approach improves data consistency and reduces storage costs, as datasets can be shared across various services and regions within the cloud infrastructure.

Hybrid cloud models further highlight the value of NFS integrations. Many organizations operate hybrid environments where certain workloads run in the cloud while others remain on-premises due to regulatory, security, or legacy application constraints. NFS provides a bridge between these environments, enabling on-premises servers to export NFS shares that cloud-based applications can mount over VPNs or dedicated direct connections such as AWS Direct Connect or Azure ExpressRoute. This capability supports scenarios such as cloud bursting, where temporary increases in workload demand are handled by spinning up additional resources in the cloud that still rely on accessing data stored on-premises via NFS.

Container orchestration platforms like Kubernetes frequently leverage NFS shares as persistent volumes to provide stateful storage for applications running in pods. By integrating NFS with cloud-hosted Kubernetes clusters, administrators can ensure that containers have access to shared file systems that persist across pod restarts and deployments. This is particularly useful for applications such as content management systems, media processing pipelines, or legacy applications that require POSIX-compliant file system access, which object storage services like Amazon S3 or Azure Blob Storage do not natively provide.

Security is a critical consideration when using NFS in cloud integrations. While NFS facilitates convenient file sharing, it was originally designed for trusted environments and may not offer the level of security required for public cloud deployments by default. Modern implementations often mitigate this by supporting encryption for data in transit, integrating with cloud identity and access management systems, and implementing export restrictions that limit which clients can mount the file systems. Additionally, some cloud NFS services integrate with native security frameworks such as AWS Identity and Access Management (IAM) or Azure Active Directory, allowing for granular access controls and audit logging to monitor data access activities.

Performance optimization is another focus area when deploying NFS in cloud environments. Cloud providers often design their NFS services to be regionally distributed, highly available, and capable of scaling throughput based on demand. However, administrators must still consider factors such as network latency, instance types, and workload patterns when architecting solutions. For high-performance workloads, selecting appropriate instance types with enhanced networking capabilities and tuning NFS mount options—such as adjusting read and write buffer sizes—can yield significant improvements in file system performance. Additionally, the distributed nature of many cloud environments means that care must be taken to minimize cross-region data access, which can introduce unnecessary latency and costs.

The integration of NFS with cloud storage services ultimately enhances flexibility and accelerates cloud adoption for organizations with diverse infrastructure requirements. By allowing teams to retain familiar NFS workflows while taking advantage of the scalability and operational benefits of the cloud, NFS serves as a key enabler of modern hybrid and multi-cloud strategies. Whether supporting legacy applications, cloud-native workloads, or complex data pipelines, NFS remains a reliable and effective solution for unifying storage access across distributed computing environments. As cloud providers continue to expand their support for NFS and related file services, organizations will find even greater opportunities to leverage this protocol in building efficient, scalable, and secure cloud-integrated storage architectures.

NFS over VPN and Encrypted Channels

Deploying Network File System (NFS) over Virtual Private Networks (VPNs) and encrypted channels has become a critical strategy for organizations seeking to balance the convenience and flexibility of NFS with the security requirements of modern distributed environments. While NFS has long been a staple in enterprise networks for providing shared file access, its original design assumed trusted, internal networks where security threats were minimal. As organizations increasingly connect remote sites, cloud resources, and mobile workforces, securing NFS traffic has become a paramount concern. Utilizing VPNs and encryption provides a necessary layer of protection for sensitive data that travels across untrusted or public networks.

NFS operates by enabling client machines to mount remote file systems hosted on NFS servers over an IP-based network, allowing seamless file sharing and access. In a local area network (LAN) or private datacenter setting, this model offers simplicity and high performance. However, when NFS traffic must traverse wide area networks (WANs) or the public internet, it becomes susceptible to a variety of security risks. These include man-in-the-middle attacks, eavesdropping, and unauthorized data access. NFS, particularly older versions like NFSv3, does not provide built-in encryption for data in transit, leaving transmitted files, user credentials, and metadata exposed to interception.

To mitigate these risks, organizations often employ VPNs to create secure, encrypted tunnels between geographically separated networks. A VPN encapsulates and encrypts all network traffic between endpoints, ensuring that NFS operations such as file reads, writes, and directory listings occur within a protected channel. Whether using site-to-site VPNs to link branch offices to a central datacenter or remote-access VPNs to enable individual users to securely mount NFS shares from external locations, VPNs play a critical role in extending

NFS beyond the confines of private networks while preserving confidentiality and integrity.

Several VPN technologies are commonly used in conjunction with NFS. IPsec-based VPNs, for example, are a widely adopted standard that provides strong encryption and authentication at the IP layer. IPsec can be implemented in transport mode for securing specific communication pairs or in tunnel mode to secure all traffic between two networks. Another popular option is SSL/TLS-based VPNs, such as OpenVPN, which operate at higher layers and provide additional flexibility, including compatibility with firewalls and network address translation (NAT) environments. WireGuard, a modern VPN protocol, has gained traction for its simplicity, speed, and strong cryptographic foundations, making it an attractive option for securing NFS traffic across public networks.

In addition to leveraging VPNs, organizations can secure NFS traffic by configuring the protocol to operate over encrypted channels directly. NFSv4 introduced several improvements over its predecessors, including built-in support for stronger authentication and integrity protection through the integration of RPCSEC_GSS and Kerberos. By configuring NFSv4 with Kerberos authentication and enforcing the use of integrity or privacy services, administrators can ensure that NFS operations are authenticated, tamper-proof, and optionally encrypted end-to-end. This is particularly useful in enterprise environments where NFS traffic may remain within a trusted internal network but still require protection against insider threats or accidental data exposure.

Nevertheless, deploying NFS over VPN or encrypted channels introduces performance considerations that must be carefully managed. Encryption and encapsulation add processing overhead to both NFS servers and clients, potentially impacting throughput and latency. The degree of performance impact depends on several factors, including the encryption algorithms used, hardware capabilities of the systems involved, and the nature of the workloads. For instance, transferring large files or conducting intensive I/O operations over an encrypted VPN tunnel may result in slower performance compared to unencrypted NFS traffic on a local network. To address this, organizations often employ hardware acceleration, such as AES-NI instruction sets found in modern CPUs, or deploy dedicated VPN appliances to offload encryption tasks.

Another consideration is the choice of network architecture when implementing NFS over VPN. Site-to-site VPNs are well-suited for linking entire networks and supporting multiple NFS clients that require access to centralized storage, such as in branch office scenarios. In contrast, remote-access VPNs are more appropriate for individual users who need secure, ad-hoc access to NFS shares while working remotely. Hybrid models can also be employed, where core business units use site-to-site VPNs, while mobile or contract workers connect via remote-access VPNs, all accessing the same NFS infrastructure securely.

Firewall configuration and network segmentation play a supporting role in enhancing the security of NFS over VPN deployments. Since NFS relies on several ports and protocols, including TCP and UDP port 2049, as well as auxiliary services like portmapper (in NFSv3), careful firewall rule definition is essential. When combined with VPNs, administrators can restrict NFS service exposure exclusively to VPN tunnels, ensuring that no NFS ports are accessible from the public internet. Additionally, isolating NFS servers and related services on dedicated VLANs or network segments within the protected VPN infrastructure further reduces the risk of lateral movement by malicious actors.

In multi-cloud and hybrid cloud environments, NFS over VPN becomes even more critical. Organizations frequently need to connect on-premises datacenters to cloud-hosted virtual private clouds (VPCs) where NFS servers or clients reside. In such cases, cloud providers typically offer native VPN services, such as AWS VPN, Azure VPN Gateway, or Google Cloud VPN, which enable secure tunnels between on-premises infrastructure and cloud resources. By routing NFS traffic through these encrypted channels, organizations can create secure hybrid storage architectures, allowing cloud-hosted applications to access on-premises NFS shares or vice versa.

Moreover, NFS over VPN is increasingly relevant in containerized environments and DevOps workflows. For example, Kubernetes clusters deployed across different cloud regions or on-premises and cloud locations can mount NFS shares via VPN-protected tunnels to ensure secure access to shared storage for containerized applications. This enables teams to deploy stateful workloads with confidence, knowing that sensitive data traversing between cluster nodes and NFS storage endpoints is safeguarded against unauthorized interception.

As organizations adopt zero-trust security models, additional layers of security are often integrated into NFS over VPN deployments. Zero-trust principles advocate for verifying every connection and transaction, regardless of network location. Combining VPN encryption with strict NFS export controls, multifactor authentication, and continuous monitoring ensures a defense-in-depth approach. Security Information and Event Management (SIEM) systems can also be configured to log and alert on unusual NFS activity patterns, further enhancing situational awareness and threat detection.

While VPNs and encryption technologies strengthen the security posture of NFS deployments, they must be complemented by operational best practices. Regular patching of NFS servers, VPN endpoints, and underlying operating systems is essential to address vulnerabilities. Similarly, conducting regular security audits and penetration testing of NFS over VPN implementations can uncover potential misconfigurations or weaknesses before they are exploited by attackers.

The combination of NFS with VPNs and encrypted channels represents a powerful solution for organizations looking to extend secure file-sharing capabilities beyond traditional network perimeters. It enables geographically dispersed teams and hybrid environments to safely access centralized storage, fostering collaboration and operational efficiency without compromising data security. By thoughtfully designing and maintaining these systems, organizations can achieve the benefits of NFS's flexibility and ease of use while aligning with modern cybersecurity expectations.

Diagnosing Network Bottlenecks in NFS

Diagnosing network bottlenecks in Network File System (NFS) environments is a crucial task for system administrators and network engineers who are responsible for ensuring optimal performance of shared storage across distributed systems. NFS, despite its widespread use and reliability, can be sensitive to various network conditions due to its reliance on consistent and efficient network communication between clients and servers. Performance issues can arise for many reasons, including bandwidth limitations, latency, packet loss, or misconfigurations at different layers of the infrastructure. Identifying and addressing these bottlenecks requires a systematic approach that combines network diagnostics, server and client monitoring, and an understanding of how NFS interacts with the underlying network.

One of the most common symptoms of a network bottleneck in an NFS environment is slow file access. Users may experience delays when opening, reading, or writing files stored on NFS-mounted directories. These delays can be sporadic or constant, depending on the severity and nature of the bottleneck. To begin diagnosing the issue, it is essential to assess the overall health and capacity of the network infrastructure, starting with bandwidth utilization. High bandwidth consumption caused by competing traffic or large data transfers can easily saturate links and limit the throughput available for NFS traffic. Tools like iftop, iperf, or nload can be deployed on both NFS servers and clients to measure real-time network usage and identify whether saturation is occurring on specific network interfaces.

Latency is another critical factor that can degrade NFS performance. Unlike local file systems, NFS requires multiple round-trip communications between clients and servers to complete common file operations. Excessive latency, even when bandwidth is sufficient, can severely slow down these operations, particularly for applications that perform many small file transactions. Measuring latency using tools like ping or traceroute helps identify whether there are delays introduced by the network path between NFS servers and clients. Issues such as long physical distances between sites, suboptimal routing, or overloaded intermediate network devices like routers and switches can introduce additional latency.

Packet loss is another frequent cause of NFS bottlenecks, as NFS traffic typically uses TCP, which is sensitive to lost packets. TCP retransmits lost segments and employs congestion control algorithms that reduce transmission rates when loss is detected, leading to reduced throughput. Diagnosing packet loss involves running tools like mtr (My Traceroute) or using network hardware monitoring to identify where in the path packets are being dropped. Common culprits include overloaded network links, faulty hardware, or misconfigured Quality of Service (QoS) policies that deprioritize NFS traffic in favor of other applications.

Jumbo frames, while beneficial in some high-performance environments, can also be a source of bottlenecks if not uniformly configured across the network. Jumbo frames are Ethernet frames with payloads larger than the standard 1500 bytes, typically set to 9000 bytes. If some switches or interfaces do not support jumbo frames while others do, the resulting mismatch can cause fragmentation or even dropped packets, negatively affecting NFS performance. Ensuring consistent Maximum Transmission Unit (MTU) settings across all devices along the NFS communication path is a necessary step in troubleshooting this type of issue.

Another layer to consider when diagnosing bottlenecks is server-side and client-side resource utilization. Even when network conditions appear normal, bottlenecks may result from CPU or memory contention on the NFS server or client machines. High CPU usage on the NFS server, caused by processes like encryption overhead, excessive context switching, or poorly optimized applications, can delay NFS responses, making it appear as if there is a network issue. Monitoring server performance using tools like top, htop, or vmstat can provide insights into whether the server is struggling under load. On the client side, resource-hungry applications competing for network and disk I/O can also contribute to performance degradation when accessing NFS shares.

NFS-specific parameters and configuration also play a role in perceived network bottlenecks. For example, NFS clients typically employ attribute caching to reduce the number of server calls, but overly aggressive caching settings can result in stale data being presented to users or applications. On the other hand, conservative cache settings can increase the number of NFS operations, placing additional stress on the network and server. Mount options such as rsize and wsize, which determine the read and write buffer sizes for NFS operations, can directly affect performance. Larger buffer sizes reduce the number of round trips required for large data transfers, but they must be balanced against the capabilities of the network and hardware to avoid fragmentation or excessive memory usage.

Monitoring NFS protocol activity using tools like nfsstat on both client and server systems provides detailed metrics about the number and type of NFS operations being performed, as well as retransmissions and error rates. This data helps pinpoint whether the bottleneck is caused by excessive NFS requests, a high number of retransmissions due to network issues, or slow server-side processing of client requests. Capturing and analyzing network traffic using packet sniffers like tcpdump or Wireshark allows administrators to inspect NFS packets directly, helping to identify anomalies such as delayed responses, duplicate acknowledgments, or congestion signals from TCP.

In virtualized and cloud environments, diagnosing NFS bottlenecks introduces additional complexity. Virtual machines and containers often share physical network interfaces and storage backends, making them susceptible to resource contention. In such cases, bottlenecks may occur due to oversubscription of virtualized network adapters or shared storage arrays, requiring administrators to review hypervisor-level or container orchestration metrics to identify hotspots. Tools native to cloud providers, such as AWS CloudWatch or Azure Monitor, can provide valuable insights into network and storage utilization patterns that affect NFS performance.

Network design also plays a fundamental role in NFS performance. A flat network topology with limited switching capacity may become overwhelmed as the number of NFS clients grows. Introducing hierarchical designs with dedicated storage networks or leveraging technologies like VLANs and QoS policies can help segment and prioritize NFS traffic, reducing the likelihood of contention with other services such as voice or video conferencing.

Ultimately, diagnosing network bottlenecks in NFS environments requires a holistic approach that takes into account all components of the system: the client, the server, and the network fabric that connects them. By systematically gathering and analyzing data from each layer, administrators can uncover the root causes of slow NFS performance and implement targeted optimizations. Whether the solution involves upgrading network links, tuning NFS parameters, or balancing workloads across additional servers, identifying and resolving bottlenecks ensures that NFS continues to deliver the reliable, high-performance file sharing expected in demanding enterprise and cloud-based infrastructures.

Migrating Data with NFS

Migrating data using Network File System (NFS) is a common and reliable approach in enterprise environments where large datasets must be moved between systems, storage arrays, or even data centers. NFS provides a convenient method for mounting remote file systems and copying data across networks, allowing administrators to execute migrations without the need for physically transporting disks or interrupting service availability for extended periods. The flexibility of NFS makes it particularly well-suited for migrations between heterogeneous systems, as it enables Linux, Unix, macOS, and even Windows systems with NFS client support to access shared file systems during the migration process.

Data migration projects often arise due to various operational needs, such as hardware upgrades, data center consolidations, cloud adoption, or transitioning to new storage architectures. When NFS is used as part of the migration strategy, it allows the source data to be mounted directly onto the destination system as a remote file system. This means files can be transferred over the network while maintaining file-level access control and compatibility with existing applications. Administrators typically initiate such migrations by mounting the NFS export from the source system onto the target system, after which data can be copied using traditional file transfer commands such as cp, rsync, or tar.

One of the advantages of migrating data with NFS is that it minimizes downtime in production environments. Since NFS supports concurrent read and write access, administrators can often perform migrations while systems remain online, reducing disruption for users. For example, administrators can begin by copying the bulk of static files ahead of time and then synchronize any changes made during the migration window using incremental transfer tools like rsync. This staged approach ensures that the final cutover can be executed quickly, with only a short service interruption required for final synchronization and switchover to the new storage.

However, NFS-based migrations require careful planning to ensure consistency, data integrity, and security throughout the process. Before beginning the migration, administrators must verify that NFS services are correctly configured on both the source and destination systems, including confirming export settings, file permissions, and network access controls. Ensuring that the target system has adequate storage capacity and performance to handle the incoming data is also critical. Additionally, verifying compatibility between the NFS versions in use is important, as some systems may default to older versions like NFSv3 while others prefer NFSv4, which includes support for advanced features such as stronger authentication and ACLs.

Network performance plays a pivotal role in the success of data migrations over NFS. Since data is transferred across the network, bottlenecks such as limited bandwidth, high latency, or packet loss can significantly slow the process. To mitigate these risks, organizations often perform migrations during off-peak hours or implement Quality of Service (QoS) policies to prioritize NFS traffic. Where possible, administrators may leverage high-speed network links, such as 10GbE or faster connections, to accelerate data transfers. Tools like iperf and nload can assist in monitoring and optimizing network performance before and during the migration.

The choice of data transfer tool also influences the efficiency of an NFS-based migration. Rsync is a particularly popular option because of its ability to perform incremental transfers, which reduces the amount of data that needs to be copied during the final synchronization phase. Rsync's checksum-based comparison ensures that only changed files or file blocks are transferred, saving time and bandwidth. For massive datasets, parallelization techniques such as running multiple rsync instances in parallel or using tools like GNU Parallel can further speed up the process. In scenarios where preserving file permissions, timestamps, and symbolic links is critical, rsync and tar both offer options to maintain these attributes during the migration.

Data integrity verification is a crucial step in any migration process. After the transfer is complete, administrators should perform validation checks to ensure that all data has been copied successfully and remains uncorrupted. This often involves generating checksums (e.g., using md5sum or sha256sum) for both the source and destination datasets and comparing them to detect discrepancies. In large-scale environments, automated scripts may be used to verify file counts, sizes, and metadata consistency across both systems.

Security considerations are equally important when migrating data with NFS, especially when traversing untrusted or public networks. NFSv3, while widely used, does not encrypt data in transit, exposing sensitive information to potential interception. To mitigate this risk, administrators may implement IPsec tunnels or VPNs to secure the NFS traffic between the source and destination. Alternatively, organizations can choose NFSv4 with Kerberos authentication and encryption to enforce secure data transfers natively. Strict firewall rules and network segmentation should also be enforced to limit NFS access only to authorized systems participating in the migration.

In hybrid or multi-cloud environments, NFS continues to be a valuable tool for data migrations. Organizations migrating workloads to the cloud often mount on-premises NFS exports directly onto cloud-based virtual machines or file storage services that support NFS. For instance, a company migrating from an on-premises data center to Amazon Web Services (AWS) may mount its existing NFS shares onto an EC2 instance or an Amazon Elastic File System (EFS) mount point, facilitating seamless data transfers to cloud storage. This approach supports hybrid cloud strategies where applications in the cloud can continue accessing legacy datasets hosted on-premises until full migration is complete.

Challenges during NFS migrations can also arise when dealing with differences in file system semantics or operating system behavior. For example, case sensitivity in file names may differ between systems, leading to potential conflicts or overwrites. Special file types such as device files, sockets, and pipes may require additional handling depending on the destination system's file system type and capabilities. To mitigate these issues, administrators should perform thorough assessments of both the source and destination environments and implement scripts or manual processes to resolve conflicts as they arise.

Another factor to consider is the user and group ID (UID/GID) mappings between source and destination systems. Since Unix-like systems rely on UIDs and GIDs to enforce file permissions, discrepancies in ID mappings can result in permission issues after the migration. Ensuring that both environments share consistent UID/GID mappings or implementing ID translation mechanisms is necessary to maintain proper access controls once the data has been migrated.

Post-migration tasks often include updating NFS mounts in application configurations, reconfiguring clients to point to the new NFS server, and validating application functionality against the migrated data. Additionally, administrators may conduct performance tuning on the destination system to optimize NFS mount options, network settings, and storage parameters to meet production requirements. This ensures that the new environment not only replicates the original functionality but also provides improved reliability, scalability, or performance as intended by the migration project.

Migrating data with NFS remains a practical and widely adopted method due to its compatibility, ease of use, and ability to facilitate both incremental and large-scale transfers. By following best practices and carefully managing each step of the migration process, organizations can achieve successful outcomes while minimizing risks to data integrity, security, and operational continuity.

Scaling NFS in Enterprise Environments

Scaling NFS in enterprise environments requires a thoughtful approach to design, deployment, and ongoing optimization to meet the increasing demands of users and applications. As businesses grow and their data needs expand, the challenges associated with providing fast, reliable, and secure access to shared file systems also increase. NFS, as a widely used protocol for network-based file sharing, must be carefully scaled to support hundreds or thousands of clients, massive datasets, and high-performance applications without becoming a bottleneck. To achieve this, administrators must consider a range of factors, from hardware and network architecture to protocol optimizations and redundancy strategies.

In a small or medium-sized environment, a single NFS server may be sufficient to serve the file-sharing needs of a limited number of clients. However, as the number of users and the volume of data grow, this architecture can quickly reach its limits. The NFS server may become overwhelmed by the sheer number of concurrent requests, leading to slower response times and degraded user experience. One of the first steps in scaling NFS is to address server capacity. This involves upgrading the NFS server's hardware resources, including CPU, memory, and storage subsystems. Modern NFS servers deployed in enterprise environments often feature high-performance multi-core processors, large amounts of RAM for caching frequently accessed data, and fast storage arrays, such as NVMe or SSD-based storage.

Another critical component of scaling NFS is network design. NFS relies on network connectivity between clients and servers, making network throughput and latency key performance factors. In large enterprise environments, it is common to implement dedicated storage networks that separate NFS traffic from general-purpose application and user traffic. This can be accomplished using dedicated VLANs, isolated network segments, or even physically separate network interfaces exclusively reserved for storage communication. Additionally, upgrading network infrastructure to 10GbE, 25GbE, or even faster connections helps prevent network bottlenecks that can limit NFS performance as client numbers and data transfer rates increase.

To support larger workloads, many enterprises adopt load-balancing techniques. Instead of relying on a single NFS server, administrators can deploy multiple NFS servers to distribute client requests and balance the load across several nodes. This can be achieved by partitioning datasets and assigning them to different NFS servers or by using DNS round-robin configurations to distribute client connections. For more advanced scenarios, enterprises may implement clustered NFS server architectures that provide both load balancing and high availability. Solutions such as NFS-Ganesha or distributed file systems like GlusterFS and CephFS, which offer NFS gateways, are popular choices for environments that demand horizontal scalability and redundancy.

Parallel NFS (pNFS) is another technology that addresses the need for scaling NFS in high-demand environments. As part of the NFSv4.1 specification, pNFS allows clients to access data across multiple storage nodes simultaneously, significantly reducing the load on a single NFS server and improving overall performance. By distributing I/O operations in parallel across multiple servers or storage devices, pNFS can support greater throughput and lower latency compared to traditional NFS setups. This is particularly advantageous in enterprise environments where workloads such as media rendering, scientific computing, or big data analytics require massive parallel access to shared datasets.

Storage backend architecture also plays a vital role in scaling NFS. Enterprises often deploy NFS servers backed by enterprise-grade storage arrays capable of handling thousands of IOPS (Input/Output Operations Per Second) with minimal latency. Integrating NFS with Storage Area Networks (SANs) or software-defined storage platforms ensures that the underlying storage infrastructure can keep pace with the demands of a growing client base. Features such as tiered storage, where frequently accessed data resides on high-performance SSDs while less frequently used data is moved to slower, cost-effective disks, help optimize storage efficiency and performance.

Caching is another technique used to enhance NFS scalability. On the server side, memory-based caching mechanisms reduce disk I/O by retaining frequently accessed data in RAM, improving response times for repeat requests. On the client side, attribute caching and read-ahead caching help minimize the number of requests sent to the server, reducing network overhead and server load. Fine-tuning caching parameters on both ends is critical, as overly aggressive caching can lead to issues with data consistency, while conservative caching may negate performance benefits.

Security considerations become more complex as NFS scales across larger enterprise environments. Ensuring secure access control without impacting performance is a balancing act. Enterprises must implement robust authentication and authorization mechanisms, such as NFSv4 with Kerberos integration, to safeguard sensitive data. Access control lists (ACLs) can be used to enforce fine-grained permissions on shared directories. At the network level, enterprises often deploy firewall rules, private networks, and VPNs to limit NFS exposure and protect traffic as it traverses internal and external networks.

Monitoring and automation are also essential for maintaining performance and availability as NFS scales. Enterprise environments rely on monitoring tools that provide real-time visibility into server health, network traffic, storage utilization, and client behavior. Tools such as Prometheus, Grafana, and Nagios allow administrators to set up alerts for potential issues like high CPU usage, disk saturation, or slow client response times. Automated scaling mechanisms, including infrastructure-as-code (IaC) practices and orchestration tools like Ansible, Terraform, or Kubernetes, help deploy and configure NFS servers and clients consistently across large environments, ensuring scalability without introducing manual errors.

High availability (HA) configurations become increasingly important as NFS scales in enterprise contexts. NFS servers must be designed to handle hardware failures, maintenance windows, and unexpected outages without disrupting client access. HA strategies include deploying redundant servers in active-active or active-passive configurations, using shared storage to ensure that failover nodes have immediate access to the same file systems. Clustered NFS implementations can automate failover and recovery, minimizing downtime and maintaining service continuity even when failures occur.

Compliance and data governance requirements must also be considered when scaling NFS. Enterprise environments often operate under regulatory frameworks that mandate specific data protection, audit logging, and retention policies. Scaled NFS environments must be capable of enforcing these policies across a large number of clients and datasets. Centralized logging, access auditing, and integration with security information and event management (SIEM) systems are common practices to ensure compliance while maintaining efficient operations.

Scaling NFS in enterprise environments is a multifaceted effort that requires coordination across hardware, network infrastructure, software configurations, and operational processes. By focusing on distributed architectures, high-performance networking, robust security, and proactive monitoring, organizations can ensure that NFS continues to meet the demands of large-scale users and applications. As data volumes grow and workloads become more complex, the ability to scale NFS effectively becomes not only a technical requirement but a strategic advantage for maintaining productivity and business continuity.

NFS and File System Quotas

Implementing file system quotas in Network File System (NFS) environments is essential for maintaining control over shared storage resources, especially in multi-user or enterprise scenarios where data growth can quickly spiral out of control. NFS provides seamless file sharing across networks, allowing multiple clients to access and manipulate data on centralized servers. However, without restrictions, individual users or applications could consume excessive amounts of disk space, leading to storage shortages, degraded performance, and potential system outages. File system quotas are an effective way to prevent these issues by enforcing limits on the amount of storage a user, group, or project can consume within the NFS-exported file systems.

Quotas are typically implemented at the file system level on the NFS server, where administrators define hard and soft limits for users and groups. A hard limit represents the absolute maximum amount of space a user can consume, beyond which no additional data can be written. A soft limit, on the other hand, provides some flexibility by allowing users to temporarily exceed their quota for a defined grace period. This dual mechanism encourages users to manage their space usage proactively while giving them time to adjust without immediate disruption.

In NFS environments, the server is responsible for managing quota enforcement, as the file system resides on the server itself. Clients that mount NFS shares are unaware of the underlying quota mechanisms, as the enforcement occurs transparently during file operations such as creating or modifying files. This server-centric model ensures centralized control, simplifying quota administration even in large-scale environments where hundreds or thousands of clients may access the same shared storage.

For file systems such as ext4, XFS, and ZFS, quota support is integrated and can be enabled with specific options when the file system is created or later modified. Once quotas are enabled, tools like edquota, setquota, and quotaon are used to configure and activate the limits. Administrators can define quotas on a per-user or per-group basis, depending on the needs of the organization. In environments where departments or project teams share storage, group quotas are particularly useful for allocating fair usage across collective workloads.

One of the challenges in NFS and quota management arises from the nature of distributed environments. Users may access NFS shares from multiple clients, which can lead to discrepancies if quotas are not properly monitored and enforced. The solution lies in deploying robust quota reporting tools and automating regular quota checks. Commands like repquota generate detailed reports that show usage statistics against defined limits, while the quota command, when run on client systems, queries the NFS server to provide users with real-time feedback on their space usage.

Beyond basic space quotas, modern file systems offer additional capabilities, such as inode quotas, which limit the number of files and directories a user can create. This is particularly useful in scenarios where users or applications create large numbers of small files, which can exhaust inodes before disk space itself runs out. By setting inode quotas alongside space quotas, administrators can safeguard the file system against inode exhaustion, which would otherwise prevent new files from being created, even if space is still available.

In enterprise NFS environments, quota management is often integrated into broader storage policies. For instance, administrators may enforce different quota levels based on user roles, project priorities, or business units. Mission-critical applications might be allocated larger quotas to ensure sufficient capacity for production workloads, while development and testing environments may operate under tighter limits to encourage efficient storage usage. Policies may also incorporate automated alerting systems, where users receive notifications via email or system messages when they approach or exceed their soft limits, prompting them to clean up unnecessary files before the hard limit is reached.

Quota enforcement also ties into larger organizational objectives such as cost control, performance optimization, and data governance. By limiting the amount of data each user or group can store, enterprises can avoid the need for constant storage expansion, reducing capital expenditures and improving return on investment for existing infrastructure. Controlled storage environments also reduce backup and replication times, as smaller datasets require fewer resources for data protection tasks. In addition, well-implemented quota systems help with compliance initiatives by ensuring that data retention policies are respected and that storage sprawl is minimized.

Performance considerations must also be accounted for when deploying quotas in NFS environments. In some file systems, enabling quotas introduces slight overhead, as the system must check quota compliance during each write operation. However, modern implementations have optimized these processes to minimize performance impacts, particularly on high-performance file systems like XFS and ZFS. Administrators should benchmark storage performance both before and after enabling quotas to evaluate any changes and fine-tune configurations accordingly.

In hybrid and cloud-integrated NFS deployments, quota enforcement remains a key concern. Many cloud-based NFS services, such as Amazon Elastic File System (EFS) or Azure NetApp Files, allow administrators to simulate quota functionality by segmenting storage into multiple volumes or directories and applying different service tiers or storage limits. While traditional Unix-style quotas may not be natively supported by all cloud offerings, combining NFS shares with policies enforced at the cloud platform level, such as IAM permissions or storage class restrictions, can help emulate similar control mechanisms.

For multi-tenant environments, where NFS serves a wide variety of teams or external customers, quotas become even more critical. Without quotas, one tenant could monopolize shared resources, impacting other tenants and degrading overall system performance. Service providers offering NFS-based storage as part of their infrastructure-as-a-service (IaaS) or platform-as-a-service (PaaS) offerings often rely on strict quota enforcement to maintain service level agreements (SLAs) and ensure equitable resource distribution among users.

Automating quota management is increasingly common in modern NFS environments. Administrators may employ scripts or configuration management tools such as Ansible or Puppet to automate the creation and adjustment of quotas based on user onboarding and offboarding processes, project lifecycles, or changes in business priorities. Automation ensures that quota policies remain consistent across the organization and reduces the risk of manual configuration errors.

Lastly, education and communication are essential components of successful quota implementation. Users must be aware of quota policies, their current usage, and best practices for managing disk space. Providing accessible documentation, usage reports, and self-service tools for checking quotas empowers users to take ownership of their storage consumption, fostering a culture of responsibility and efficiency within the organization.

The combination of NFS and file system quotas creates a powerful framework for managing shared storage in enterprise environments. By balancing flexibility with control, administrators can ensure that NFS-based file systems remain performant, cost-effective, and compliant with organizational policies, even as data volumes and user demands continue to grow.

Load Balancing for NFS

Load balancing for Network File System (NFS) environments is a critical strategy in ensuring optimal performance, reliability, and scalability, particularly in enterprise settings where multiple clients rely on shared storage systems for daily operations. NFS, by design, allows multiple client machines to access file systems hosted on a centralized server over a network. However, as the number of clients and volume of data increases, a single NFS server can quickly become overwhelmed, leading to performance degradation, longer response times, and system bottlenecks. Implementing load balancing mechanisms helps distribute client requests more evenly across multiple servers or network paths, preventing overutilization of any single resource and ensuring a smooth user experience.

In traditional NFS deployments, one of the most common performance issues is server-side overload. A single NFS server handling hundreds or thousands of simultaneous client requests may struggle with CPU, memory, or disk I/O saturation, especially during peak periods when many users are reading from or writing to shared directories. To address this challenge, administrators often deploy multiple NFS servers that share the storage workload. One basic method for distributing client load is using DNS round-robin, where multiple NFS server IP addresses are returned in a cyclic manner when clients resolve a domain name associated with the NFS service. This approach provides a rudimentary form of load balancing by directing different clients to different servers based on DNS responses.

While DNS round-robin can offer some level of load distribution, it lacks real intelligence or awareness of server health and current load levels. A more robust approach involves deploying a network load balancer or NFS proxy that actively monitors the state of backend NFS servers and routes client requests to the optimal node. These load balancers can be hardware appliances or software-based solutions and typically operate at the IP or transport layer, balancing incoming NFS traffic across multiple servers based on factors such as server health, CPU usage, network bandwidth, or number of active connections. By directing requests away from overloaded servers and towards underutilized ones, network load balancers significantly improve the efficiency and resilience of NFS environments.

Another common technique is to design the storage architecture using a multi-server model where different datasets are distributed across several NFS servers. For example, home directories for employees in different departments or regions may reside on separate NFS servers. Clients are configured to mount specific exports based on their departmental or regional affiliation, reducing contention for server resources. This method, sometimes referred to as static partitioning, ensures that each NFS server handles only a subset of the total workload, preventing a single point of saturation and simplifying capacity planning.

A more dynamic and scalable approach to NFS load balancing is the implementation of clustered NFS solutions. Clustered NFS environments involve multiple NFS servers working together as a unified system, often leveraging shared storage backends such as SANs or distributed file systems. Solutions like NFS-Ganesha, combined with cluster managers such as Pacemaker and Corosync, provide an active-active or active-passive architecture where NFS services are automatically distributed across nodes based on client demand or failover scenarios. In an active-active configuration, all NFS servers actively handle client requests simultaneously, whereas in an active-passive setup, standby nodes are ready to take over if a primary server fails. This clustered approach not only balances the load but also enhances availability and fault tolerance.

Parallel NFS (pNFS), introduced as part of the NFSv4.1 specification, represents a significant advancement in load balancing capabilities for NFS. pNFS separates the metadata server from the data servers, allowing NFS clients to retrieve file system metadata from a centralized metadata server while accessing data directly from multiple storage servers in parallel. This distributed data access model reduces bottlenecks on single servers and maximizes network and storage throughput. Clients benefit from parallel I/O paths, which is particularly advantageous for workloads requiring high throughput and low latency, such as video rendering, scientific simulations, or big data analytics.

Beyond server-side considerations, network load balancing also plays a key role in distributing NFS traffic. Enterprises often use techniques like Equal-Cost Multi-Path (ECMP) routing to balance traffic across multiple network paths between NFS clients and servers. ECMP takes advantage of multiple available routes with equal cost, automatically balancing network traffic loads and providing redundancy in case of path failures. Combined with high-speed networking infrastructure, such as 10GbE or 25GbE links and properly configured VLANs, ECMP helps ensure that NFS traffic flows smoothly even under heavy load conditions.

Client-side configurations also contribute to effective load balancing. Administrators can design client mount configurations to distribute traffic by assigning different mount points to different NFS servers. Additionally, automounters such as autofs can be configured with weighted priorities or dynamic mount rules to direct specific types of file access to specific servers. In some cases, administrators implement client-side load balancing scripts that monitor server performance metrics and dynamically remount NFS exports to the least-loaded server available. These strategies help optimize resource utilization and improve client performance, especially in environments with fluctuating workloads.

Monitoring and analytics are crucial components of any NFS load balancing strategy. Enterprises typically deploy monitoring solutions such as Prometheus, Zabbix, or Grafana to track NFS server metrics, network performance, and client connection patterns in real-time. By analyzing this data, administrators can detect imbalances, identify underperforming nodes, and adjust load balancing policies or infrastructure accordingly. Proactive capacity planning, driven by historical data trends, enables IT teams to scale NFS environments efficiently as demands grow, ensuring consistent performance and service quality.

Security must also be factored into load balancing architectures. As NFS servers and clients communicate over the network, administrators should ensure that load balancers and proxies do not inadvertently bypass authentication and access control policies. Implementing NFSv4 with Kerberos authentication, restricting NFS exports to specific IP ranges, and isolating NFS traffic on secure networks are essential practices. Additionally, ensuring that the load balancing layer itself is highly available and secured against threats is critical, as compromising this layer could impact the entire NFS infrastructure.

In cloud and hybrid environments, load balancing for NFS can leverage native cloud services. Cloud providers such as AWS, Azure, and Google

Cloud offer managed load balancing solutions that can be integrated with NFS-compatible services like Amazon EFS or Azure NetApp Files. These services simplify the deployment of scalable NFS environments by providing built-in redundancy, health checks, and automatic scaling features. Cloud-native load balancers can route NFS traffic across multiple availability zones or regions, enhancing fault tolerance and supporting global workloads.

Ultimately, load balancing for NFS environments is an ongoing process that evolves alongside organizational needs and technological advancements. By carefully designing load balancing architectures that account for server performance, network efficiency, client behavior, and security, enterprises can build NFS infrastructures capable of handling large-scale, high-demand workloads while maintaining performance, reliability, and user satisfaction.

NFS and Disaster Recovery Planning

Network File System (NFS) plays a pivotal role in disaster recovery (DR) planning for organizations that rely on shared network storage to support critical business operations. Disaster recovery refers to the strategies and processes put in place to ensure that an organization can quickly resume normal activities following an unexpected disruption, such as hardware failure, cyberattacks, natural disasters, or human error. NFS, as a protocol that enables clients to access files stored on a centralized server over a network, is often a key component of IT infrastructures and must be carefully integrated into any comprehensive DR plan.

The first step in incorporating NFS into disaster recovery planning involves identifying and prioritizing critical data and services that depend on NFS exports. Many organizations use NFS to store business-critical data such as user home directories, shared project files, application data, and databases. As such, any interruption to NFS services can halt workflows, delay projects, or impact customer-facing applications. Understanding which file systems are essential and how NFS services are consumed by different departments or applications is crucial for defining recovery point objectives (RPO) and recovery time objectives (RTO). RPO determines how much data loss is acceptable in terms of time, while RTO defines how quickly services must be restored to minimize business impact.

Once critical NFS-dependent resources have been identified, organizations must implement robust backup and replication strategies to ensure data availability during a disaster scenario. Regular backups of NFS-exported file systems are a foundational element of DR planning. These backups should be stored in offsite or cloud-based locations to protect against data center-level failures. Tools such as rsync, Bacula, or enterprise backup solutions can be used to automate backups of NFS-mounted file systems. In addition to full backups, incremental or differential backups are often used to reduce data transfer volumes and backup windows while still providing effective data protection.

Replication is another key strategy for disaster recovery in NFS environments. Synchronous replication mirrors data to a secondary NFS server in real time, ensuring that both primary and secondary servers contain identical data. While synchronous replication guarantees minimal data loss, it requires high-bandwidth, low-latency connections between the primary and secondary sites. Asynchronous replication, on the other hand, introduces a slight delay but reduces the burden on network resources and is better suited for geographically distant disaster recovery sites. Technologies such as DRBD (Distributed Replicated Block Device) or storage-level replication provided by SANs or distributed file systems can be integrated with NFS servers to facilitate real-time or near-real-time data synchronization.

High availability (HA) configurations complement disaster recovery efforts by providing redundancy within the same site. Implementing clustered NFS servers using tools such as Pacemaker and Corosync allows for failover between nodes, ensuring that if one NFS server fails, another can take over with minimal service interruption. This setup addresses local hardware failures but must be paired with offsite disaster recovery strategies to cover larger-scale disasters. Combining HA with geographic replication enables organizations to build resilient architectures that protect against both localized and site-wide outages.

Testing and validation are essential elements of disaster recovery planning for NFS. An untested DR plan is likely to fail when most needed. Organizations must regularly perform simulated failovers, backup restoration tests, and replication integrity checks to verify that data can be recovered as expected. Testing also uncovers hidden dependencies, such as application configurations that hard-code IP addresses or mount points, which could impede a smooth transition to a secondary NFS server during a disaster. These exercises should involve both IT staff and business stakeholders to ensure alignment on expectations and to refine recovery procedures over time.

Automation can significantly enhance NFS disaster recovery workflows. Configuration management tools such as Ansible, Puppet, or Chef can automate the deployment and configuration of NFS servers, reducing the time required to provision new servers during a recovery scenario. Similarly, infrastructure-as-code (IaC) practices enable rapid provisioning of cloud-based recovery environments, where NFS shares can be quickly recreated using predefined templates and scripts. Automating these processes not only speeds up recovery efforts but also reduces the risk of human error during high-pressure disaster situations.

Security considerations must also be integrated into NFS disaster recovery planning. Ensuring that data replicated or backed up for DR purposes is encrypted both in transit and at rest is critical for protecting sensitive information. NFS traffic itself, particularly in older versions like NFSv3, is not encrypted by default, so additional measures such as VPNs or IPsec tunnels should be employed when replicating data between geographically separated sites. In NFSv4 environments, Kerberos authentication and encryption options should be fully utilized. Furthermore, access controls and firewall rules at DR sites must be consistent with production environments to prevent unauthorized access during or after a disaster.

In cloud-integrated environments, disaster recovery strategies for NFS are increasingly leveraging cloud-native services. Organizations can back up or replicate NFS data to cloud object storage solutions such as Amazon S3, Azure Blob Storage, or Google Cloud Storage. During a disaster, cloud-based compute instances can mount cloud-managed file systems such as Amazon EFS or Azure NetApp Files to restore services. This hybrid model provides flexibility and scalability, allowing businesses to recover from disasters without the need for a fully provisioned secondary data center.

Business continuity planning must go hand-in-hand with disaster recovery efforts. Beyond restoring technical services such as NFS, organizations must ensure that employees, partners, and customers can continue accessing the resources they need. This may involve redirecting users to alternative access points, updating DNS records to point to DR sites, and ensuring remote work solutions are in place. For instance, if employees access NFS shares through virtual desktop infrastructure (VDI) or remote file access tools, these systems must also be factored into the DR plan.

Documentation is a cornerstone of successful NFS disaster recovery planning. Clear and comprehensive documentation should include step-by-step recovery procedures, roles and responsibilities, configuration details for both primary and DR sites, and contact information for key personnel. Documentation should be reviewed and updated regularly to reflect changes in infrastructure, applications, and business requirements. In high-pressure disaster scenarios, this documentation becomes a critical resource for guiding recovery efforts and ensuring consistency.

Ultimately, NFS is deeply embedded in the storage architectures of many organizations, making its inclusion in disaster recovery planning a necessity. By combining backup, replication, high availability, automation, and security best practices, businesses can safeguard their NFS environments against a wide range of disruptive events. A well-designed and thoroughly tested DR strategy ensures that data remains available, operations resume quickly, and business impact is minimized when disaster strikes.

Leveraging NFS with NAS Appliances

Leveraging Network File System (NFS) with Network Attached Storage (NAS) appliances has become a fundamental practice in modern IT environments, providing organizations with a scalable, flexible, and efficient solution for shared storage needs. NAS appliances are purpose-built devices that connect to a network and provide centralized storage services to multiple clients. By integrating NFS as the primary file-sharing protocol, NAS appliances can deliver seamless access to files across diverse operating systems and platforms, making them a preferred choice for businesses of all sizes seeking to streamline data access and storage management.

NFS, as a protocol, is designed to facilitate file-level access to shared directories over IP networks, allowing client systems to mount remote file systems and interact with them as if they were local. When combined with NAS appliances, NFS extends these capabilities by leveraging the hardware, software, and storage management features offered by the NAS device. Modern NAS appliances are equipped with high-performance processors, large memory capacities, and robust disk subsystems, which enable them to efficiently handle concurrent access from dozens or even hundreds of NFS clients. This allows organizations to consolidate their file storage infrastructure onto a centralized NAS platform, reducing complexity and improving manageability.

One of the key benefits of using NFS with NAS appliances is the ease of deployment. Most NAS solutions come with pre-installed NFS server software and intuitive graphical interfaces for configuring and managing NFS exports. Administrators can quickly create shared directories, define export rules, and assign permissions without requiring deep expertise in Linux or Unix system administration. The simplicity of NAS configuration accelerates the deployment process, enabling businesses to provision shared storage for departments, teams, or applications in a matter of minutes. Additionally, many NAS systems integrate with directory services such as LDAP or Active Directory, allowing organizations to apply existing user and group access policies to NFS shares.

Performance is another important advantage when leveraging NFS with NAS appliances. Enterprise-grade NAS devices are optimized for high-throughput and low-latency storage operations. They often include features such as SSD caching, tiered storage, and intelligent data placement algorithms that enhance performance for frequently accessed files. By tuning NFS-specific parameters such as read and write buffer sizes or enabling asynchronous writes, administrators can further optimize performance based on workload characteristics. NAS appliances also support multiple network interfaces with link aggregation or bonding options, providing additional network bandwidth and redundancy to handle high-volume NFS traffic.

Scalability is a critical factor in enterprise environments, and NAS appliances paired with NFS excel in this area. As storage requirements grow, administrators can expand NAS capacity by adding additional disks or enclosures, often without downtime. Many NAS solutions support scale-out architectures, allowing organizations to deploy multiple NAS nodes that work together as a single storage pool while providing additional NFS endpoints. This horizontal scalability is ideal for environments with rapidly growing datasets, such as video production studios, scientific research facilities, or large software development teams, where storage demands can increase unpredictably.

NAS appliances also contribute to enhanced data protection and reliability when used with NFS. Many devices are equipped with hardware-based RAID controllers that provide protection against disk failures by distributing data redundantly across multiple drives. Snapshot capabilities allow administrators to create point-in-time copies of file systems, which can be used for quick recovery in case of accidental deletions or data corruption. Additionally, NAS appliances often include built-in backup integration and replication features, enabling NFS shares to be synchronized to remote locations or cloud services for disaster recovery purposes. These features help organizations meet business continuity and compliance requirements while ensuring that critical data remains protected.

Leveraging NFS with NAS appliances also supports diverse and dynamic workflows across various industries. In media and entertainment, for example, production teams rely on high-performance NFS shares hosted on NAS appliances to store large video files, audio assets, and project files. Editors, animators, and designers working from different workstations or remote locations can access the same shared datasets in real time, improving collaboration and productivity. In scientific research, NFS shares hosted on NAS devices are used to store experimental data, simulation results, and analysis scripts, providing researchers with centralized access to critical resources while facilitating data sharing among collaborators.

Hybrid IT environments further benefit from integrating NFS with NAS appliances. Many organizations operate a combination of on-premises infrastructure and cloud services, and NAS devices often bridge the gap between these environments. Some NAS appliances offer built-in cloud connectivity, enabling seamless tiering of older or less frequently accessed files to cloud storage platforms such as Amazon S3, Azure Blob Storage, or Google Cloud Storage. This hybrid model allows businesses to maintain high-performance NFS access for active data while optimizing costs by offloading cold data to more economical cloud storage tiers.

Security is a crucial aspect when deploying NFS on NAS appliances. Enterprise-grade NAS devices typically provide advanced security features such as encrypted file systems, secure NFSv4 implementation with Kerberos authentication, and granular access control lists (ACLs). Administrators can restrict NFS exports to specific IP addresses or subnets, reducing the risk of unauthorized access. Furthermore, auditing and logging capabilities available on many NAS platforms allow organizations to track file access and changes, supporting compliance with regulations such as GDPR, HIPAA, or SOX.

Automation and integration with modern IT tools also enhance the value of using NFS with NAS appliances. Many NAS vendors provide RESTful APIs, CLI tools, or integrations with orchestration platforms such as Kubernetes, Ansible, or VMware vSphere. These capabilities allow administrators to automate the creation and management of NFS exports, dynamically provision storage for virtual machines or containers, and integrate NAS-based NFS shares into broader DevOps pipelines. Automated workflows reduce the manual effort required to manage storage and ensure consistency across environments.

In addition to technical benefits, leveraging NFS with NAS appliances offers significant cost-efficiency advantages. Compared to deploying and maintaining traditional file servers on general-purpose hardware, NAS appliances deliver purpose-built storage solutions that reduce the total cost of ownership (TCO). They consolidate storage management, simplify backup and disaster recovery processes, and minimize the need for additional server infrastructure, saving on hardware, licensing, and administrative overhead. Many NAS solutions are also available in modular designs, allowing businesses to start with smaller configurations and expand as needed, making them suitable for both small businesses and large enterprises.

Ultimately, integrating NFS with NAS appliances creates a powerful and flexible file-sharing solution that meets the diverse needs of modern organizations. From providing centralized storage for collaborative teams to supporting performance-intensive workloads and hybrid cloud models, NAS appliances equipped with NFS capabilities remain a cornerstone of networked storage strategies. By combining ease of use, scalability, robust security, and high availability, this integration helps businesses achieve greater operational efficiency, data protection, and agility in today's fast-evolving digital landscape.

Distributed File Systems: Beyond NFS

While Network File System (NFS) has long been a cornerstone for shared file access in enterprise environments, the evolution of IT infrastructures and the increasing complexity of modern workloads have given rise to distributed file systems that go beyond the traditional capabilities of NFS. Distributed file systems are designed to provide scalable, reliable, and highly available storage across geographically dispersed locations, cloud platforms, and hybrid environments. Unlike the conventional client-server model of NFS, which often relies on a single centralized server or cluster of servers, distributed file systems offer decentralized architectures that distribute data and metadata across multiple nodes. This approach addresses many of the limitations associated with NFS, particularly when it comes to handling large-scale, high-performance, or globally distributed workloads.

One of the most widely recognized distributed file systems is Hadoop Distributed File System (HDFS), which was developed as part of the Apache Hadoop project. HDFS is specifically designed to store and process vast amounts of data across clusters of commodity hardware.

It is optimized for high-throughput access to large files rather than low-latency access to small files, making it ideal for big data analytics, data lakes, and machine learning pipelines. HDFS splits large files into blocks and distributes them across multiple nodes, with built-in replication to ensure fault tolerance. When one node fails, the system can still access data from replicated blocks on other nodes, providing resilience and continuous availability.

Another prominent distributed file system is GlusterFS, an open-source solution that aggregates storage resources from multiple servers into a single global namespace. GlusterFS provides a POSIX-compliant file system that is accessed over traditional protocols like NFS, SMB, or its native Gluster protocol. It offers features such as data replication, erasure coding, and geo-replication, making it suitable for organizations that need scalable storage with high availability across multiple sites. Unlike NFS, which relies on a central server or clustered architecture, GlusterFS operates on a peer-to-peer model, where all participating nodes contribute to both data storage and metadata operations. This eliminates single points of failure and allows for easier scaling by simply adding more nodes to the storage cluster.

Ceph is another distributed file system that has gained significant traction in enterprise and cloud-native environments. Ceph's architecture is based on the Reliable Autonomic Distributed Object Store (RADOS), which provides object, block, and file storage within a unified system. CephFS, the file system layer of Ceph, offers POSIX-compliant access to data stored in the RADOS cluster. What sets Ceph apart from NFS is its ability to deliver high scalability and fault tolerance without requiring proprietary hardware or dedicated metadata servers. Ceph dynamically distributes both data and metadata across its storage nodes, providing balanced workloads and automatic self-healing in the event of node failures. Ceph is widely used in OpenStack clouds and Kubernetes clusters, where it provides persistent storage for virtual machines and containers.

Lustre is another distributed file system that has become synonymous with high-performance computing (HPC) environments. Designed for large-scale scientific computing, research facilities, and supercomputers, Lustre can manage petabytes of data and serve thousands of clients simultaneously. It excels in scenarios where applications require parallel access to massive datasets with minimal latency. Lustre divides its architecture into metadata servers (MDS) and object storage servers (OSS), separating metadata management from actual data storage. This allows for greater parallelism and significantly improves I/O performance compared to traditional NFS systems. Due to its specialized design, Lustre is often deployed in environments where computational speed and data throughput are paramount, such as genome sequencing, weather modeling, or oil and gas simulations.

While distributed file systems like HDFS, GlusterFS, Ceph, and Lustre provide advanced capabilities that surpass many aspects of NFS, each solution also introduces unique challenges. For example, distributed file systems often require more complex deployment and management compared to the relatively simple setup of an NFS server. They may also introduce higher learning curves for administrators and necessitate dedicated resources for monitoring, tuning, and maintenance. Additionally, application compatibility can sometimes be a concern, as not all legacy applications are designed to interact with newer distributed storage backends.

Despite these challenges, the advantages of distributed file systems make them indispensable for modern IT infrastructures. They provide inherent redundancy by distributing data across multiple physical locations, reducing the risk of data loss due to hardware failures or network outages. They also offer elasticity, allowing organizations to scale their storage environments horizontally by adding more nodes or cloud resources without reconfiguring the entire system. Distributed file systems are highly adaptable to hybrid and multi-cloud strategies, enabling data to be stored across on-premises datacenters and public cloud platforms while maintaining a unified namespace and seamless data access.

Moreover, distributed file systems are increasingly integrated with cloud-native technologies such as container orchestration platforms. For example, Kubernetes supports distributed file systems like CephFS and GlusterFS as persistent storage providers for stateful workloads running in pods. These integrations allow distributed file systems to play a central role in cloud-native application architectures, providing reliable storage for microservices, databases, and other critical components.

The rise of object-based storage solutions further complements the distributed file system landscape. While traditional distributed file systems provide file-level access, object storage systems like Amazon S3, MinIO, and OpenStack Swift focus on storing data as objects within flat address spaces. Object storage is well-suited for applications that require scalable storage for unstructured data, such as media files, backups, and big data archives. Many distributed file systems, including Ceph, offer object storage gateways, allowing organizations to leverage both file and object storage paradigms within a single infrastructure.

Enterprises are also exploring hybrid models where distributed file systems operate alongside traditional NFS servers. In such scenarios, NFS may continue to serve legacy applications and lightweight workloads, while distributed file systems handle more demanding or modern use cases. By strategically combining both technologies, organizations can optimize their storage environments for performance, cost-efficiency, and future scalability.

The transition beyond NFS to distributed file systems is driven by the need to meet the demands of data-intensive industries and applications. Whether supporting scientific research, media production, cloud-native applications, or global business operations, distributed file systems provide the resilience, scalability, and performance that modern organizations require. Their decentralized architectures eliminate traditional bottlenecks and single points of failure, making them an essential component of next-generation storage solutions. As data volumes continue to grow exponentially and workloads become more complex, distributed file systems will play an increasingly vital role in shaping the future of enterprise and cloud storage architectures.

NFS Integration with Active Directory

Integrating Network File System (NFS) with Active Directory (AD) is a crucial task for organizations that operate mixed environments where Linux and Unix servers must coexist with Windows-based infrastructure. Active Directory serves as the backbone of identity and access management for many enterprises, providing centralized authentication, authorization, and user management. By integrating NFS with Active Directory, organizations can streamline user access to shared file systems, enforce consistent access control policies, and simplify administration across both Unix-like and Windows systems.

Traditionally, NFS was designed for Unix-based environments, relying on User IDs (UIDs) and Group IDs (GIDs) to manage file ownership and permissions. In contrast, Windows environments managed by Active Directory use Security Identifiers (SIDs) and access control lists (ACLs) to handle security and permissions. This fundamental difference creates a challenge when integrating NFS servers, which operate in the UID/GID paradigm, with an Active Directory domain where users and groups are defined by SIDs. Without proper integration, administrators risk misaligned user permissions, inconsistent access controls, and a fragmented user experience.

The core objective of NFS and Active Directory integration is to map Unix-style UIDs and GIDs to their corresponding AD user and group accounts. This is commonly achieved using a component known as Identity Mapping or ID mapping. One of the most popular solutions is to use services such as Winbind from the Samba project, System Security Services Daemon (SSSD), or LDAP integration to pull user information from Active Directory and translate it into Unix-compatible identifiers. SSSD, in particular, has gained popularity due to its versatility and native support in many modern Linux distributions. It acts as an intermediary between NFS servers and the AD domain, allowing Linux systems to retrieve user and group information directly from Active Directory without requiring complex configurations.

Once identity mapping is configured, NFS servers can assign appropriate file ownership and enforce access control based on AD-defined users and groups. This seamless mapping allows users to access

NFS-mounted file systems using their familiar AD credentials, without the need for separate Unix accounts or duplicated user databases. Consistency in user identities across both environments is essential to prevent permission conflicts, unauthorized access, or data loss.

A common method for configuring this integration is to set up the NFS server as an LDAP client that queries Active Directory's LDAP interface. Administrators configure nsswitch.conf to include LDAP as a source for user and group information, while also setting up Kerberos authentication to align with Active Directory's single sign-on (SSO) model. Kerberos enables secure, ticket-based authentication, allowing users to access NFS shares without repeatedly entering passwords once they are authenticated in the domain. NFSv4, which includes native support for Kerberos via RPCSEC_GSS, is the recommended version when integrating with Active Directory, as it ensures encrypted and authenticated communication between NFS clients and servers.

Integrating NFS with Active Directory also simplifies access management and auditing. System administrators can create and manage users, groups, and policies from a single pane of glass within Active Directory, ensuring that access control policies applied to Windows file shares are consistent with those applied to NFS exports. For example, AD group membership can be leveraged to control access to specific NFS-mounted directories, with permissions enforced by the NFS server using the mapped GIDs. Additionally, this approach supports enterprise compliance and auditing requirements, as all access logs can be correlated to AD accounts, providing clearer accountability and traceability across the organization's file-sharing infrastructure.

When configuring NFS exports in an Active Directory-integrated environment, administrators must pay close attention to file system permissions and export options. Using options such as sec=krb5 or sec=krb5i in the NFS export configuration ensures that only Kerberos-authenticated clients can access the shares, providing a secure and unified authentication experience across both Unix and Windows clients. Furthermore, NFSv4's support for ACLs allows for more granular access control compared to the traditional Unix permission model. Administrators can apply ACLs directly on NFS-mounted directories to mirror the fine-grained access policies commonly enforced in Windows environments.

Another advantage of this integration is improved user experience. Employees working on Linux workstations can access NFS shares using their existing AD accounts, while those using Windows clients may access the same shared data through SMB/CIFS or other AD-integrated services. This interoperability reduces friction for users and simplifies collaboration across teams using different operating systems. Developers, designers, analysts, and administrators can all work within the same shared storage framework without worrying about inconsistent file permissions or identity mismatches.

Challenges do exist when integrating NFS with Active Directory, particularly when dealing with UID and GID consistency across multiple Unix systems. In environments where local Unix users are still present alongside AD users, administrators must ensure there are no conflicting UID or GID assignments between local and domain accounts. Properly scoping ID mapping ranges and using tools like wbinfo or getent to verify mappings can help resolve these conflicts. Additionally, some legacy applications or older NFS clients may lack full support for NFSv4 and Kerberos, requiring special considerations or upgrades to ensure compatibility.

The integration also has performance considerations. Depending on the size of the Active Directory domain and the frequency of LDAP queries, systems using SSSD or Winbind may experience increased lookup times, especially during periods of heavy load. Caching mechanisms built into SSSD can mitigate this by temporarily storing user and group information, reducing the dependency on constant LDAP lookups. However, administrators must configure appropriate cache expiration policies to balance performance with data accuracy.

Security remains a top priority throughout the integration process. Administrators should harden the NFS server by disabling unused services, restricting exports to specific AD users or groups, and isolating NFS traffic on secure networks. Implementing firewall rules to block unauthorized IP ranges, enforcing TLS encryption for LDAP queries, and applying Kerberos policies that require strong encryption further enhance the security posture of the integrated environment.

In hybrid cloud environments, NFS and Active Directory integration can extend beyond on-premises infrastructure. Organizations using cloud-based services such as AWS Managed Microsoft AD or Azure Active Directory Domain Services can configure cloud-hosted NFS servers or NAS appliances to authenticate against these directory services. This allows enterprises to maintain a unified identity management system across cloud and on-premises workloads, supporting secure and consistent access control across geographically distributed users.

Integrating NFS with Active Directory streamlines identity management, simplifies permissions control, and bridges the gap between Unix and Windows ecosystems. This integration enables organizations to centralize authentication and authorization processes while providing users with a consistent and secure experience when accessing shared file systems. By aligning NFS and Active Directory, businesses can improve operational efficiency, reduce administrative overhead, and strengthen security across their entire storage infrastructure.

Automation with NFS using Scripts

Automation has become a fundamental part of modern IT operations, and Network File System (NFS) environments are no exception. Automating NFS-related tasks using scripts enables administrators to streamline workflows, reduce human error, and improve the efficiency and consistency of routine operations. From mounting NFS shares to managing permissions and monitoring usage, scripting is a powerful tool that brings flexibility and control to environments where NFS is widely deployed across servers, workstations, or cloud instances.

One of the most common use cases for automation in NFS environments is the automated mounting and unmounting of NFS shares across multiple client systems. In traditional environments, administrators would manually edit the /etc/fstab file or use mount commands on each system to configure NFS mounts. However, when managing hundreds or thousands of servers or workstations, this manual approach becomes impractical and prone to inconsistencies.

By leveraging shell scripts, administrators can automate the deployment of NFS mounts across large fleets of machines. For example, a simple Bash script can query a centralized configuration file or database that contains NFS server details and export paths, and then automatically mount the appropriate NFS shares on each client system based on predefined criteria such as server role, department, or geographic location.

In addition to mounting shares, automation scripts are frequently used to manage NFS exports on the server side. Administrators often need to create, update, or remove NFS exports as business needs change. By automating the generation of /etc/exports configurations and triggering the exportfs command to refresh exports, scripts can quickly and consistently apply changes across multiple NFS servers. These scripts may include logic to dynamically set export options such as read-only or read-write access, root squash settings, and client access restrictions based on IP ranges or hostnames. Automating this process ensures that NFS exports remain aligned with security policies and operational requirements without requiring manual intervention for each change.

Automation also plays a crucial role in managing permissions and ownership on NFS-mounted directories. Since NFS clients rely on consistent user and group IDs (UIDs and GIDs) for enforcing file system permissions, discrepancies between systems can cause access issues or security vulnerabilities. Scripts can be used to synchronize UID and GID mappings across client systems by querying central identity management services, updating /etc/passwd and /etc/group files, or using tools such as SSSD to maintain consistent identity resolution. Furthermore, automation scripts can be scheduled to periodically audit and correct file and directory permissions on NFS shares, ensuring that sensitive data is protected and that users have appropriate access rights.

Another area where automation enhances NFS operations is in backup and data protection workflows. Administrators can write scripts that automate the process of backing up data stored on NFS shares to remote storage or cloud services. These scripts may use tools like rsync, tar, or custom logic to perform incremental or full backups, manage retention policies, and generate reports on backup success or failure.

For instance, a nightly script could back up an NFS-exported directory to an offsite location, verify the integrity of the backup using checksums, and notify administrators of the results via email or a messaging platform. Automation reduces the risk of missed backups and ensures that critical data is consistently protected.

Monitoring and alerting are essential components of NFS management that can also benefit from scripting. Scripts can be created to monitor key performance metrics such as NFS server load, mount point availability, or disk space usage on NFS-mounted directories. Using simple tools like df, iostat, or nfsstat within scripts, administrators can gather real-time information about the health of NFS services. These scripts can trigger automated alerts when thresholds are exceeded, such as low disk space or high latency, allowing administrators to proactively address issues before they impact end users. Additionally, logs generated by NFS daemons can be parsed and analyzed by scripts to detect anomalies or security events, such as unauthorized access attempts or repeated mount failures.

In dynamic environments such as those powered by cloud or container orchestration platforms, automation scripts are particularly valuable. For instance, in Kubernetes environments where stateful workloads require persistent storage, administrators can automate the provisioning and mounting of NFS-backed persistent volumes using scripts or integration with the Kubernetes API. Similarly, Infrastructure-as-Code (IaC) tools like Terraform or Ansible often rely on custom scripts to configure NFS servers, deploy export configurations, and automate the provisioning of storage resources for cloud-native applications.

Scripting languages such as Bash, Python, and Perl are commonly used to automate NFS tasks due to their versatility and integration with Unix-like systems. Python, for example, offers modules such as os, subprocess, and paramiko, which enable administrators to automate NFS operations locally or across remote systems via SSH. More complex automation workflows can incorporate logic to handle edge cases, perform error handling, and log detailed execution outputs for auditing purposes. Scripts can be integrated with cron or systemd timers to execute on a scheduled basis, ensuring regular maintenance of NFS infrastructure.

Automation with NFS also extends to the deployment and scaling of NFS servers themselves. Scripts can be designed to automate server provisioning, configure network interfaces, install necessary NFS packages, and apply tuning parameters such as adjusting the number of NFS threads or enabling asynchronous I/O for improved performance. These server automation scripts can be integrated into continuous deployment pipelines, enabling rapid scaling of NFS infrastructure in response to increased storage demands or changes in business priorities.

Security automation is another important consideration. Scripts can be developed to regularly audit NFS export configurations for misconfigurations, ensure that secure NFSv4 features such as Kerberos authentication are enforced, and automatically apply updates to NFS-related software to address security vulnerabilities. Automating these security tasks reduces the risk of configuration drift, improves compliance with organizational security policies, and helps ensure that NFS services remain protected against emerging threats.

Finally, automation brings significant benefits to disaster recovery planning in NFS environments. Scripts can automate the replication of NFS data to offsite locations, validate data integrity, and generate recovery documentation that outlines the steps required to restore services in the event of a disaster. By scripting these procedures, organizations can reduce recovery time objectives (RTOs) and ensure that critical storage services can be restored quickly and reliably.

Automation with NFS using scripts is essential for building efficient, resilient, and secure storage environments. By eliminating repetitive manual tasks, reducing the risk of errors, and enabling rapid scaling and recovery, automation empowers IT teams to manage NFS infrastructure with greater agility and confidence. As organizations continue to embrace DevOps practices and modernize their infrastructure, scripting remains a foundational skill that drives operational excellence in NFS environments.

Understanding NFSv4 ACLs

NFSv4 introduced Access Control Lists (ACLs) as a powerful and flexible mechanism for managing file and directory permissions beyond the traditional Unix permission model. In earlier versions of NFS, access control was limited to the basic read, write, and execute permissions associated with users, groups, and others, enforced through standard Unix file permissions. While sufficient for many use cases, this model lacked the granularity needed in more complex environments, especially those requiring fine-tuned permissions across diverse user bases. NFSv4 ACLs address this limitation by providing a richer and more granular access control system, similar to the permissions model found in Windows environments.

An NFSv4 ACL is essentially a list of Access Control Entries (ACEs) attached to a file or directory. Each ACE defines specific permissions for a user or group, along with whether those permissions should be allowed or denied. Unlike traditional Unix permissions, which can only assign one set of permissions per file for the owner, group, and others, NFSv4 ACLs allow multiple entries for different users and groups, enabling administrators to implement more sophisticated access control policies. This makes NFSv4 ACLs highly valuable in shared environments where multiple teams, departments, or individuals require distinct levels of access to the same file system resources.

Each ACE consists of several components. The principal identifies the user or group to which the entry applies. This could be a specific user, a group, or a predefined entity like "everyone" or "authenticated users." The type defines whether the permissions specified are to be allowed or denied. The permissions field specifies which actions are controlled by the ACE, such as read data, write data, execute, delete, or modify ACL. There is also a flag field, which controls how the ACE behaves in relation to directories, such as whether it should be inherited by newly created files or subdirectories.

One of the most powerful aspects of NFSv4 ACLs is their ability to support inheritance, which allows administrators to define ACLs on a directory that will automatically propagate to files and subdirectories created within it. This is particularly useful for large directory trees where maintaining consistent access control is important but manually configuring permissions on every individual object would be inefficient and error-prone. By applying inheritable ACEs at the root of a directory structure, administrators can ensure that the same access control policies are automatically applied to all nested content.

The permissions provided by NFSv4 ACLs are more granular than standard Unix permissions. For example, NFSv4 ACLs allow for separation between the ability to read file attributes and read file contents, or between writing data and modifying file metadata. This allows administrators to create fine-tuned policies where, for example, a user can read a file but cannot modify its timestamp or permissions, or where another user may have the ability to create files in a directory but not delete existing ones. This level of control is particularly useful in collaborative environments or shared file systems where sensitive data must be protected from accidental or unauthorized modifications.

NFSv4 ACLs also help bridge compatibility gaps between Unix and Windows systems. In mixed environments where Windows clients interact with NFS shares, administrators often need to enforce permissions that align with Windows security expectations. NFSv4 ACLs offer a similar model to NTFS ACLs, making it easier to map Windows file permissions to NFS shares without losing access control granularity. This compatibility improves user experience and security in hybrid environments, where cross-platform file sharing is a common requirement.

Configuring and managing NFSv4 ACLs is done using tools such as nfs4_setfacl and nfs4_getfacl, which are analogous to the setfacl and getfacl tools used for POSIX ACLs. These tools allow administrators to view, modify, and remove ACLs directly on NFS-mounted file systems. The nfs4_getfacl command displays the ACL entries for a specified file or directory, showing the principals, permission bits, and inheritance flags associated with each ACE. The nfs4_setfacl command enables the creation or modification of these entries, supporting operations such as adding a new ACE to grant read access to a specific user or removing an ACE that previously allowed write access to a particular group.

When working with NFSv4 ACLs, administrators must understand how they interact with traditional Unix permissions. In NFSv4, ACLs and Unix permissions coexist, but the ACL is the primary enforcement mechanism when it is present. If a file or directory has an associated NFSv4 ACL, the traditional mode bits (e.g., 755 or 644) act as a simplified view of the ACL's effective permissions but do not override the more detailed ACL configuration. This means that changes made using chmod may not affect the actual access control enforced by the ACL, and administrators must manage permissions through ACL tools for accurate control.

NFSv4 ACLs also introduce the concept of canonical and non-canonical forms. A canonical ACL follows a specific order of ACEs, typically placing deny entries before allow entries, which ensures predictable and secure behavior. Non-canonical ACLs, where allow entries precede deny entries, can lead to unintended permission grants if not carefully managed. Administrators should consistently structure ACLs in canonical order to prevent potential security risks, especially in multi-user environments where overlapping permissions can occur.

Performance considerations should also be noted when implementing NFSv4 ACLs. Although ACLs provide greater flexibility, each file access request involves additional checks to evaluate the ACL, which can introduce slight overhead compared to traditional Unix permissions. However, this impact is generally minimal in modern NFS servers and is outweighed by the benefits of precise access control. Administrators should nonetheless monitor performance in high-traffic environments and consider optimizing NFS server configurations, such as enabling attribute caching, to mitigate potential slowdowns.

Security is inherently improved with NFSv4 ACLs due to the ability to enforce the principle of least privilege more effectively. By precisely controlling which users and groups have access to specific actions on files and directories, organizations can reduce the risk of accidental data modification, unauthorized file deletion, or privilege escalation. This is particularly important in regulated industries such as healthcare, finance, or government, where compliance requirements demand strict access controls and detailed auditing of file access events.

Auditing is further supported by the visibility that NFSv4 ACLs provide into the permissions structure of the file system. Administrators can generate ACL reports using scripts that leverage nfs4_getfacl, documenting current access policies for compliance purposes or internal reviews. Combined with logging tools that capture NFS access logs, these reports contribute to a complete audit trail that can be used for security analysis or forensic investigations.

Understanding and effectively using NFSv4 ACLs is crucial for modern enterprises seeking advanced access control capabilities within their NFS environments. The ability to define detailed, inheritable permissions tailored to specific users and groups enables organizations to secure shared file systems with a level of precision that exceeds traditional Unix permissions, while also ensuring compatibility with mixed OS environments and complex organizational workflows. As data governance and security requirements continue to evolve, NFSv4 ACLs will remain a vital tool in the administrator's toolkit.

Real-World NFS Use Cases

Network File System (NFS) has remained a cornerstone technology in many industries for decades, largely due to its simplicity, reliability, and compatibility with a wide range of operating systems. As organizations continue to adopt hybrid IT infrastructures and modernize their workflows, NFS continues to provide value across various sectors. Its ability to provide file-level access over a network in a transparent and efficient manner makes it a popular choice for shared storage environments. Real-world use cases demonstrate how NFS underpins critical operations, enabling organizations to manage data effectively, support collaboration, and enhance performance across diverse applications.

In software development environments, NFS is frequently used to support distributed teams and automate DevOps workflows. Development teams often require centralized repositories to store source code, configuration files, build artifacts, and documentation. By hosting these resources on NFS servers, teams can share and access files from multiple development machines, continuous integration servers, and testing environments. NFS facilitates rapid code sharing, enabling developers working on different platforms to collaborate in real time without worrying about transferring files manually between systems. In large enterprises, NFS is often integrated into automated build pipelines, where build servers running on virtual machines or physical hosts mount NFS exports to fetch source code, store build outputs, and manage test results.

In higher education and research institutions, NFS is a critical component in supporting academic and scientific computing environments. Universities and research labs often deploy large NFS-based storage systems to manage data generated from experiments, simulations, and research studies. In high-performance computing (HPC) clusters used for tasks such as climate modeling, bioinformatics, or particle physics, NFS servers provide centralized storage to compute nodes, allowing them to read and write data to a shared file system during parallel processing operations. Researchers benefit from the seamless access to shared datasets, eliminating the need to replicate large files across each compute node. Additionally, administrative staff leverage NFS to store student records, course materials, and other institutional documents in a secure and centralized location, making it easier to manage data at scale.

In the media and entertainment industry, NFS plays a key role in managing workflows for video production, animation, and digital content creation. Creative professionals working on video editing, visual effects, and 3D rendering projects often require access to large media files, such as high-resolution video clips, audio tracks, and project files. By using NFS to host these assets on centralized storage appliances, media teams can collaborate across multiple workstations in post-production studios. Editors, animators, and designers can access and modify project files concurrently, improving workflow efficiency and minimizing project delivery times. NFS's compatibility with non-linear editing systems (NLEs) and rendering software makes it a standard solution for shared storage in broadcast, film production, and game development studios.

Enterprise IT environments also rely heavily on NFS for server infrastructure and storage consolidation. NFS is frequently deployed to provide shared storage for application servers, database servers, and web servers operating within a data center or cloud environment. For example, web servers running content management systems (CMS) or e-commerce platforms may share assets such as website templates, media files, and customer-uploaded content over NFS-mounted directories. This approach simplifies storage management and ensures that all servers have access to a consistent data set, improving availability and scalability. In virtualized environments, hypervisors such as VMware ESXi or KVM may use NFS datastores to store virtual machine images, templates, and snapshots, streamlining storage provisioning and reducing administrative overhead.

In the healthcare sector, NFS supports critical clinical and operational workflows. Hospitals and healthcare providers handle vast amounts of sensitive patient data, including medical imaging, electronic health records (EHR), and laboratory results. NFS servers are often used to host medical imaging files generated by systems such as PACS (Picture Archiving and Communication Systems) and radiology equipment. Clinicians, radiologists, and specialists can access patient imaging studies stored on NFS shares from different workstations or departments, facilitating faster diagnosis and treatment. The scalability and interoperability of NFS allow healthcare organizations to integrate shared storage with a variety of medical devices and software platforms while maintaining compliance with data protection regulations.

In cloud and hybrid cloud architectures, NFS remains a go-to solution for enabling shared storage between on-premises systems and cloud workloads. Many cloud service providers offer NFS-compatible services, such as Amazon Elastic File System (EFS) or Azure NetApp Files, which allow businesses to mount cloud-based file systems on their virtual machines and containerized applications. Organizations migrating workloads to the cloud may continue to use NFS as the storage backend for legacy applications that require file-level access or POSIX-compliant storage. This hybrid approach allows businesses to extend existing NFS-based workflows to the cloud without disrupting operations, ensuring seamless access to data regardless of whether applications run on-premises or in public cloud environments.

Another common use case is found in manufacturing and engineering sectors, where NFS enables the management of CAD (Computer-Aided Design) and CAM (Computer-Aided Manufacturing) files. Design teams working on complex engineering projects, such as product development or industrial design, need access to large design files and project documentation stored in shared directories. NFS provides fast and consistent access to these resources, allowing teams to collaborate on product iterations, run simulations, and manage version control effectively. The ability to centralize and protect design assets while enabling distributed access is essential in reducing project timelines and maintaining product quality.

In government and defense applications, NFS is often used to support secure and mission-critical systems. Government agencies that handle sensitive data related to national security, public records, or citizen services rely on NFS servers to store and manage information in a controlled environment. NFS can be configured to integrate with strong authentication mechanisms such as Kerberos, ensuring that only authorized users and systems can access classified or sensitive information. Combined with encrypted communication channels and access control lists, NFS provides a secure and dependable solution for government data sharing requirements.

Backup and disaster recovery is another area where NFS plays a vital role. Organizations use NFS shares as targets for storing backup copies of data from production systems, providing centralized storage that can be easily integrated with backup software. For example, servers running backup agents may mount NFS shares to write incremental backups, full system images, or database dumps. In the event of a disaster, these backups can be quickly restored to new servers or cloud environments by remounting the NFS share and recovering the required data. NFS's support for snapshot and replication features further enhances disaster recovery capabilities, allowing organizations to create near-instant recovery points and replicate critical data to offsite locations for added resilience.

From software development and scientific research to media production and cloud computing, NFS continues to serve as a versatile and reliable solution across a diverse range of industries. Its ability to integrate into both legacy and modern IT environments, coupled with its flexibility in supporting varied workloads, ensures that NFS remains a crucial technology for organizations seeking efficient and scalable file sharing solutions. Real-world use cases illustrate how NFS empowers businesses to improve collaboration, streamline operations, and safeguard critical data in a rapidly evolving technological landscape.

The Future of NFS

The future of Network File System (NFS) is shaped by the evolving demands of modern IT environments, where hybrid cloud adoption, containerization, and the explosive growth of data continue to redefine how organizations approach file sharing and storage. Despite being a mature technology, NFS remains highly relevant and is undergoing significant transformation to meet the challenges of next-generation infrastructures. As enterprises push toward more distributed, scalable, and secure storage solutions, NFS is adapting through ongoing innovations, protocol enhancements, and deeper integration with emerging technologies.

One of the primary drivers influencing the future of NFS is the rapid adoption of cloud computing. Organizations are increasingly moving workloads to public and private clouds, and NFS is playing a key role in bridging on-premises systems with cloud environments. Cloud service providers are expanding their support for NFS-compatible file systems, offering fully managed services such as Amazon Elastic File System (EFS), Azure NetApp Files, and Google Cloud Filestore. These services provide the traditional benefits of NFS—such as POSIX compliance and file-level access—while delivering the scalability, elasticity, and availability features native to cloud platforms. As more businesses embrace hybrid cloud architectures, NFS will continue to serve as a critical link that unifies data access across disparate environments.

Containerization and microservices architectures are also influencing the trajectory of NFS. As containerized applications and Kubernetes clusters become more prevalent, there is a growing need for persistent, shared storage that can integrate seamlessly into these ecosystems. NFS is well-positioned to meet this demand by providing persistent storage backends for containerized workloads. Kubernetes, for example, supports NFS as a persistent volume provider, allowing containers running in pods to mount NFS shares for stateful workloads. The flexibility and simplicity of NFS make it an attractive option for developers and operations teams seeking to maintain data persistence across ephemeral container instances. As Kubernetes and

159

other container orchestration platforms evolve, the role of NFS in providing reliable storage will expand, particularly in hybrid cloud deployments where workloads shift between on-premises data centers and cloud services.

Security is a critical area of focus for the future of NFS. As cyber threats become more sophisticated and regulatory requirements grow stricter, there is an increasing emphasis on enhancing the security features of NFS deployments. Modern implementations of NFSv4 already include strong security mechanisms, such as integration with Kerberos for secure authentication and support for access control lists (ACLs) that provide granular permission management. Looking ahead, further advancements will likely include native support for end-to-end encryption of data in transit and at rest, reducing reliance on external VPNs or IPsec tunnels to protect sensitive file transfers. Additionally, new features may emerge that enable integration with modern identity and access management solutions, such as OAuth 2.0 or cloud-native IAM services, to better align NFS access control with cloud security frameworks.

Performance optimization is another key aspect shaping the future development of NFS. With the increasing demand for low-latency access to large datasets, especially in fields like big data analytics, artificial intelligence (AI), and machine learning (ML), there is a need to further improve the efficiency and speed of NFS operations. Parallel NFS (pNFS), introduced in NFSv4.1, is one such innovation that enables clients to perform direct I/O to multiple storage devices simultaneously, bypassing single-server bottlenecks. As adoption of pNFS grows, future versions of the protocol may incorporate additional enhancements to maximize parallelism and minimize overhead. Furthermore, improvements in transport layer technologies, such as leveraging RDMA (Remote Direct Memory Access) over modern high-speed networks like InfiniBand or RoCE (RDMA over Converged Ethernet), are likely to contribute to significant performance gains in NFS environments.

Automation and orchestration will also play a more prominent role in the evolution of NFS. Infrastructure-as-Code (IaC) and DevOps practices are driving the need for automated storage provisioning, configuration, and scaling. The future of NFS will include deeper integrations with orchestration tools such as Ansible, Terraform, and Kubernetes Operators, allowing NFS servers, exports, and client mounts to be fully automated and managed as code. This will enable IT teams to provision complex NFS infrastructures in minutes, ensure consistent configurations across multiple environments, and streamline disaster recovery processes by automating backup and replication workflows.

Artificial intelligence and machine learning are expected to impact NFS by enabling intelligent storage management and optimization. AI-driven analytics tools could be used to monitor NFS server performance, identify usage patterns, predict capacity bottlenecks, and recommend tuning adjustments. These insights will allow administrators to proactively address issues before they affect users, enhance the overall reliability of NFS environments, and reduce operational costs. AI-powered automation could also assist in dynamically adjusting caching strategies, allocating resources based on workload demands, and optimizing data placement in hybrid storage tiers.

Interoperability will continue to be a major focus area as enterprises seek to unify storage solutions across multiple platforms. Future iterations of NFS may offer enhanced compatibility with other distributed file systems and cloud storage services, allowing for more seamless data migration and hybrid storage models. Enterprises managing multi-cloud environments will benefit from standardized NFS APIs that facilitate integration with object storage solutions, such as Amazon S3 or Azure Blob Storage, enabling hybrid models where data can reside across file and object storage systems while remaining accessible through familiar NFS interfaces.

Sustainability and green IT initiatives are also influencing the direction of NFS development. As organizations become more conscious of their environmental impact, there is growing interest in optimizing storage systems to reduce energy consumption and carbon footprints. The future of NFS may include energy-efficient enhancements, such as intelligent power management for storage arrays, improved support for thin provisioning, and data deduplication features that reduce storage footprint. Additionally, tighter integration with cloud-native services that offer auto-scaling and on-demand resource allocation will contribute to more efficient storage utilization.

As data governance and compliance requirements grow more complex, NFS will likely evolve to support more advanced auditing and reporting capabilities. Enterprises handling sensitive data, such as personal health information (PHI) or financial records, require detailed logging and monitoring of file access and modifications. Future NFS implementations may include enhanced audit logging mechanisms that provide real-time insights into user activities, data changes, and access violations. This will support compliance with regulations such as GDPR, HIPAA, and CCPA, while helping organizations strengthen their security posture.

Ultimately, the future of NFS is one of ongoing adaptation and innovation. While newer technologies such as distributed file systems and object storage platforms have emerged to address specific storage challenges, NFS's simplicity, versatility, and broad adoption ensure its continued relevance in modern IT landscapes. As enterprises navigate the complexities of hybrid and multi-cloud environments, NFS will continue to evolve, offering new features, integrations, and optimizations that align with the demands of tomorrow's data-driven world. The enduring presence of NFS, coupled with these advancements, positions it as a key enabler of scalable, secure, and efficient storage solutions for years to come.

Compliance and Auditing with NFS

Compliance and auditing with Network File System (NFS) are critical concerns for organizations that manage sensitive data and operate in regulated industries. As NFS serves as a foundational component of many shared storage infrastructures, ensuring that it meets legal, regulatory, and internal security requirements is essential. Whether organizations are subject to government mandates such as GDPR, HIPAA, SOX, or PCI DSS, or must adhere to internal security frameworks, having effective auditing and compliance measures for NFS environments is a necessity to protect data integrity and ensure accountability.

NFS, by design, provides a flexible and efficient mechanism for sharing files over IP networks. However, its traditional Unix roots mean that early versions of NFS offered limited built-in auditing and access control features. Over time, as the protocol evolved to NFSv4, improvements such as Access Control Lists (ACLs) and support for Kerberos authentication were introduced to enhance security. Despite these advancements, ensuring regulatory compliance requires additional steps, including the deployment of comprehensive logging, auditing, and monitoring systems that capture user activities, access patterns, and configuration changes related to NFS.

A key component of compliance in NFS environments is the enforcement of strict access control policies. Modern NFS implementations allow organizations to integrate with centralized identity management systems such as LDAP, Active Directory, or Kerberos, ensuring that only authenticated and authorized users can access NFS exports. By leveraging NFSv4 ACLs, administrators can apply fine-grained permissions that regulate which users or groups can read, write, or modify specific files and directories. These access controls are fundamental in enforcing the principle of least privilege, which limits users' access rights to only what is necessary for their role, reducing the risk of unauthorized data exposure or modification.

Beyond access control, auditing is vital for tracking and documenting user activities within NFS environments. Auditing provides visibility into who accessed specific files, when the access occurred, what operations were performed, and from which systems the access originated. Collecting and analyzing this information is essential for incident response, forensic investigations, and demonstrating compliance during regulatory audits. On Linux-based NFS servers, auditing can be implemented using tools such as the Linux Auditing System (auditd). Auditd allows administrators to define audit rules that monitor file access events, including read, write, execute, and attribute changes, and log them in a centralized audit log.

The audit logs generated by auditd can be configured to capture detailed information about NFS client activities. For example, administrators can set audit rules to monitor access to critical directories exported over NFS, such as those containing customer data, financial records, or intellectual property. When users on NFS clients read, modify, or delete files in these directories, the corresponding audit entries are recorded with metadata, including the user ID, source IP address, and timestamp. This level of detail is crucial for organizations subject to regulations that require accountability for data access, such as HIPAA, which mandates audit controls to track user access to protected health information.

To manage the large volume of audit data typically generated in busy NFS environments, organizations often deploy centralized log aggregation and analysis tools. Solutions such as the ELK stack (Elasticsearch, Logstash, Kibana), Splunk, or Graylog provide powerful capabilities for collecting, indexing, and visualizing audit logs from multiple NFS servers. These tools enable security and compliance teams to create dashboards, generate automated alerts, and perform advanced searches to identify suspicious or non-compliant activities. For example, if an unauthorized user attempts to access restricted NFS shares or there are signs of data exfiltration, the system can immediately notify administrators and trigger an incident response workflow.

Another important consideration in compliance and auditing with NFS is the integrity and security of the audit data itself. Audit logs must be protected against tampering or unauthorized deletion, as their integrity is critical for legal and regulatory purposes. Organizations typically implement measures such as write-once, read-many (WORM) storage or forward audit logs to remote, hardened servers that restrict modification rights. Encryption of logs, both in transit and at rest, is also recommended to prevent unauthorized interception or access to sensitive audit information.

In addition to monitoring file access events, organizations must also audit administrative actions related to NFS server configuration and export management. Changes to the /etc/exports file, which defines the directories exported via NFS and the associated access permissions, should be logged and reviewed regularly. Automation tools such as version control systems or configuration management solutions like Ansible or Puppet can be used to track changes to configuration files, providing an auditable history of modifications. Ensuring that administrative activities are properly documented helps organizations comply with change management requirements and reduces the risk of misconfigurations that could lead to security vulnerabilities.

Data retention policies also play a role in ensuring NFS environments are compliant with regulations. Different industries may require that audit logs and access records be retained for specific periods, ranging from months to several years. By automating log rotation, archiving, and secure storage of historical audit data, organizations can meet these requirements and be prepared to present audit evidence during regulatory inspections or internal reviews.

Emerging technologies are also influencing the future of compliance and auditing with NFS. Integrating NFS environments with Security Information and Event Management (SIEM) platforms allows for advanced threat detection, correlation of events across multiple systems, and rapid incident response. SIEM solutions can combine NFS audit logs with data from firewalls, intrusion detection systems, and endpoint protection tools to provide a comprehensive view of the organization's security posture. This holistic approach helps meet compliance mandates that require organizations to demonstrate continuous monitoring and proactive threat management.

Cloud adoption adds an additional layer of complexity to NFS compliance and auditing efforts. Organizations that leverage cloud-based NFS services, such as Amazon EFS or Azure NetApp Files, must ensure that auditing capabilities extend to cloud-hosted storage. Many cloud providers offer native logging services, such as AWS CloudTrail or Azure Monitor, which can capture API calls, user actions, and configuration changes related to cloud-based NFS services. Integrating these logs into existing on-premises monitoring frameworks ensures consistent compliance and visibility across hybrid or multi-cloud environments.

Compliance and auditing in NFS environments go beyond simple access control. They require a coordinated strategy that combines technical controls, monitoring tools, secure log management, and documented policies to protect sensitive data and ensure regulatory requirements are consistently met. As data privacy regulations continue to evolve and cyber threats become more sophisticated, organizations must remain vigilant in strengthening their NFS auditing capabilities. By doing so, they not only protect their information assets but also build trust with customers, partners, and regulatory bodies, positioning themselves as responsible stewards of data.

NFS Logs and Event Management

In any organization that relies on Network File System (NFS) for centralized storage and file sharing, effective log management and event monitoring are indispensable components of a secure and resilient infrastructure. NFS, while a robust and reliable protocol for network-based file access, operates at the intersection of storage, networking, and user activity, making it a prime source of critical operational data. Properly managing and analyzing NFS logs not only assists in troubleshooting performance issues and operational anomalies but also plays a vital role in detecting security incidents, maintaining compliance, and supporting forensic investigations.

NFS servers generate logs that capture a wide range of activities, including connection attempts, file access events, service restarts, permission errors, and client mount and unmount requests. On Linux systems, the NFS server daemon (nfsd) and related components such as rpcbind or rpc.mountd typically log messages to the system's standard logging framework, which may be handled by syslog, rsyslog, or journald, depending on the distribution and configuration. These log entries are commonly written to files such as /var/log/messages, /var/log/syslog, or /var/log/secure, depending on the nature of the event. For instance, authentication or export access denials might be recorded in /var/log/secure, while general service messages appear in /var/log/messages.

One of the most important reasons to manage NFS logs effectively is to enable rapid diagnosis of operational issues. Administrators rely on NFS logs to pinpoint the root causes of client connection failures, slow file access, or permission errors. For example, if a client is unable to mount an NFS share, logs might reveal that the client IP address is not included in the export permissions or that there is a mismatch in NFS version compatibility between the client and server. Logs also provide insight into service health, such as when an NFS daemon fails to start due to configuration errors or when there are hardware-related storage issues affecting file availability. Without proper logging, identifying and resolving such issues can become a time-consuming and error-prone task.

Beyond operational troubleshooting, NFS logs are a critical component of security event management. Unauthorized access attempts, brute-force attacks against authentication services, and suspicious behavior such as unusual file access patterns or repeated permission denials can all be detected through careful log analysis. Organizations that require compliance with regulations such as HIPAA, PCI DSS, or GDPR must be able to demonstrate that they monitor and control access to sensitive data stored on NFS servers. By forwarding NFS logs to a centralized log management or Security Information and Event Management (SIEM) system, administrators can automate the detection of anomalies and generate alerts when suspicious activity is detected.

SIEM platforms such as Splunk, IBM QRadar, and Elastic's ELK stack are commonly used to aggregate NFS logs from multiple servers, correlate events with other infrastructure components, and apply advanced analytics for threat detection. By indexing NFS logs alongside data from firewalls, intrusion detection systems, and endpoint protection tools, SIEM solutions provide a comprehensive view of security events across the organization. For example, a SIEM may correlate multiple failed NFS mount attempts with abnormal login attempts on the same client machine, triggering an alert for potential credential misuse or lateral movement within the network.

Automating NFS log analysis is another key aspect of event management. While manual review of log files may suffice in small environments, larger enterprises or environments with high transaction volumes require automated log parsing and alerting systems. Log monitoring tools such as Logwatch, OSSEC, or custom scripts can be configured to scan logs for specific patterns, such as repeated export access denials or service restart loops, and automatically notify administrators via email, SMS, or incident management platforms like PagerDuty. Automating this process ensures that critical events are addressed promptly and that no significant incidents are overlooked due to human error or resource constraints.

The effectiveness of NFS log management also hinges on proper log retention and archiving policies. Depending on regulatory requirements or internal policies, organizations may need to retain logs for months or years to support audits, investigations, or legal proceedings. Logs should be securely stored in tamper-resistant formats, often by forwarding them to remote, hardened log servers or storage systems with access controls and encryption in place. Ensuring that logs are immutable and protected from unauthorized modifications is essential to maintaining their integrity and evidentiary value.

In environments with hybrid cloud deployments, NFS logs from cloud-based services such as Amazon Elastic File System (EFS) or Azure NetApp Files must be integrated with on-premises logging and SIEM systems. Cloud providers typically offer native monitoring and logging services, such as AWS CloudWatch Logs or Azure Monitor, which capture file system activity, configuration changes, and API calls related to NFS shares hosted in the cloud. Integrating these logs with centralized event management systems ensures consistent visibility and monitoring across both cloud and on-premises NFS infrastructure.

Another layer of complexity arises when dealing with distributed environments, where multiple NFS servers are deployed across different sites or regions. In such scenarios, log synchronization and correlation become critical to building a unified event management framework. Solutions like syslog-ng, Fluentd, or Graylog can be used to collect logs from geographically dispersed NFS servers, normalize the data, and forward it to a centralized SIEM platform. Time synchronization via NTP (Network Time Protocol) across all servers is also crucial to ensure accurate timestamping of events, which is essential for effective incident response and forensic analysis.

Performance monitoring is another use case where NFS logs play a valuable role. Logs can reveal trends such as increased read or write latency, NFS thread contention, or network-related issues impacting NFS throughput. By integrating log data with performance metrics collected through tools like nfsstat, iostat, or custom monitoring agents, administrators can gain a holistic understanding of the factors influencing NFS performance. Dashboards built with tools such as Grafana or Kibana can provide visualizations of these metrics, enabling real-time performance monitoring and capacity planning.

An emerging trend in NFS event management is the application of machine learning and artificial intelligence to log analysis. AI-powered tools can learn baseline behavior patterns within NFS environments and automatically identify deviations that may indicate threats or performance issues. By continuously analyzing vast amounts of log data, machine learning algorithms can reduce false positives, prioritize critical alerts, and uncover complex attack patterns that traditional rule-based systems might miss.

Incorporating NFS logs into broader incident response workflows is another best practice. Logs often provide the first indicators of a breach or system compromise. By integrating NFS log alerts with ticketing systems like ServiceNow or Jira, organizations can ensure that incidents are tracked, escalated, and resolved according to established procedures. Automated playbooks within security orchestration, automation, and response (SOAR) platforms can also be triggered by specific NFS log events, helping to contain threats and remediate vulnerabilities more quickly.

NFS logs and event management are indispensable for maintaining the operational health, security, and compliance of storage environments. As storage and networking technologies continue to evolve, the ability to capture, analyze, and act upon NFS logs will remain a critical capability for organizations seeking to protect their data, ensure service availability, and detect potential threats before they escalate into significant incidents. With the right tools and strategies in place, NFS logging becomes not just a troubleshooting resource but a foundational pillar of a resilient and secure IT infrastructure.

Troubleshooting NFS Performance Issues

Troubleshooting Network File System (NFS) performance issues is a critical task for administrators who manage shared storage in enterprise environments. NFS is designed to provide seamless file access across networks, but like any networked service, it is susceptible to a variety of performance bottlenecks that can degrade the user experience and disrupt business operations. To effectively troubleshoot NFS performance problems, administrators must adopt a methodical approach that considers factors at every layer of the system, including the network, server, client, and storage subsystems.

One of the most common symptoms of NFS performance degradation is slow file operations, such as delays when opening, reading, or writing files. This may be experienced inconsistently or may affect all clients connected to the NFS server. The first step in troubleshooting involves isolating the problem. Administrators should determine whether the issue affects a single client or is widespread across multiple clients. If only one client is affected, the root cause might reside in the client's local configuration, network path, or hardware. If multiple clients report similar issues, the problem is more likely to be found at the NFS server, network infrastructure, or storage backend.

Network performance is often a significant factor in NFS-related slowdowns. Since NFS relies on network communication to transmit file requests and data between client and server, high latency, packet loss, or bandwidth limitations can directly impact its performance. Tools such as ping, traceroute, or mtr can be used to diagnose network latency and packet loss between clients and the NFS server. Inconsistent or high round-trip times suggest congestion or routing inefficiencies that need to be addressed. Administrators may also use tools like iperf to measure available network bandwidth. If network bandwidth is saturated, deploying Quality of Service (QoS) policies or upgrading to higher-speed network interfaces such as 10GbE or 25GbE can help mitigate bottlenecks.

On the server side, NFS daemon (nfsd) performance must be examined. Running the nfsstat utility can reveal statistics such as the number of RPC calls, retransmissions, or dropped packets. A high retransmission rate often indicates network instability or insufficient NFS threads on the server to handle incoming client requests. Administrators can increase the number of nfsd threads to improve concurrency and reduce latency during periods of high demand. Additionally, reviewing system metrics with tools like vmstat, iostat, or top provides insights into CPU usage, memory consumption, and disk I/O performance on the NFS server. If the server is experiencing high CPU load or storage subsystem bottlenecks, performance will suffer across all NFS clients.

Disk I/O is a common culprit behind NFS slowdowns. If the underlying storage system supporting the NFS exports is overwhelmed with read or write operations, file access latency will increase. For environments using traditional spinning disks, slow performance may result from high disk utilization or contention within RAID arrays. Migrating frequently accessed data to solid-state drives (SSDs) or implementing tiered storage architectures can alleviate these issues. Some NFS servers also benefit from enabling write-back caching or using storage appliances with built-in cache mechanisms to accelerate disk I/O.

Client-side issues are equally important when diagnosing NFS performance problems. Clients with outdated NFS versions, suboptimal mount options, or limited hardware resources can experience degraded file access speeds. Administrators should verify that clients are running compatible versions of NFS, preferably NFSv4 or later, to take advantage of performance improvements such as compound procedures and better caching mechanisms. Mount options such as rsize and wsize, which control the read and write buffer sizes, can be adjusted to improve throughput. Larger buffer sizes can reduce the number of network round trips required for large file transfers, while smaller sizes may benefit environments with high latency or unreliable networks.

Another client-side consideration is the behavior of the local file system. If a client's local file system is nearly full or encountering its own I/O bottlenecks, NFS-mounted directories may appear sluggish even if the server is performing normally. Tools like df, du, or iotop can help administrators identify disk usage and performance issues on the client side. In addition, attribute caching can influence the responsiveness of NFS-mounted directories. Tuning the cache settings using mount options such as actimeo, acregmax, or acdirmin can balance performance and consistency according to application requirements.

NFS lock contention is another factor that can affect performance. Applications that rely heavily on file locking mechanisms may cause bottlenecks if locks are not managed efficiently. Monitoring NFS locks using tools like lslocks or examining the status of the rpc.statd and rpc.lockd daemons can reveal whether excessive locking is contributing to performance issues. Adjusting application behavior to minimize unnecessary locking or upgrading to NFSv4, which handles locking more efficiently, may resolve the problem.

Security features such as encryption and authentication can also introduce additional overhead. While Kerberos authentication with NFSv4 improves security, it may add latency, particularly in high-transaction environments where numerous authentication requests occur simultaneously. Administrators should evaluate whether the performance impact of security mechanisms is acceptable relative to the organization's security posture. For environments where performance is critical, offloading authentication to dedicated servers or adjusting Kerberos ticket lifetimes may improve responsiveness without compromising security.

Advanced troubleshooting may require capturing and analyzing network traffic between NFS clients and servers using tools like tcpdump or Wireshark. Packet captures can reveal issues such as excessive retransmissions, protocol negotiation failures, or unusually long response times from the server. Analyzing these traces helps administrators understand the underlying causes of latency or throughput issues at the protocol level, particularly in complex network environments with firewalls, load balancers, or VPN tunnels.

In highly virtualized or cloud-native environments, shared resource contention within hypervisors or container orchestration platforms can also impact NFS performance. Virtual machines or containers sharing physical network interfaces and storage backends may experience reduced throughput due to resource oversubscription. In these scenarios, isolating NFS traffic to dedicated virtual networks or deploying NFS servers on nodes with direct-attached storage and dedicated network interfaces can improve performance. Administrators may also consider container-native storage solutions that integrate NFS servers with Kubernetes, enabling more granular resource allocation and scaling.

Performance monitoring and trend analysis are essential for proactive troubleshooting. By collecting and analyzing historical performance data using tools such as Grafana, Prometheus, or Nagios, administrators can identify patterns and anticipate potential bottlenecks before they escalate. These tools provide visibility into NFS server metrics, network statistics, and storage performance, enabling IT teams to make informed decisions about capacity planning, resource allocation, and infrastructure optimization.

Troubleshooting NFS performance issues requires a holistic approach that considers all layers of the system. From client configurations and network conditions to server load and storage performance, multiple variables interact to influence how well NFS operates. By systematically investigating each component, administrators can isolate bottlenecks, implement targeted optimizations, and ensure that NFS continues to deliver reliable and responsive file sharing services across the organization's infrastructure. As NFS evolves and integrates more deeply with hybrid cloud and containerized environments, maintaining best practices in performance monitoring and tuning will be increasingly critical to achieving optimal results.

Best Practices for NFS Deployment

Deploying Network File System (NFS) in any environment, whether small-scale or enterprise-grade, requires careful planning and adherence to best practices to ensure reliability, performance, and security. NFS is a mature and widely adopted protocol that enables networked file sharing across Unix, Linux, and increasingly heterogeneous environments, including Windows and cloud platforms. While its basic implementation may seem straightforward, a well-designed NFS deployment considers not only initial setup but also scalability, fault tolerance, access control, and long-term maintainability. Applying best practices to NFS deployment ensures that it operates optimally, protects sensitive data, and supports business continuity.

The foundation of any successful NFS deployment begins with selecting the correct NFS version. While older versions like NFSv3 are still in use, NFSv4 and later versions offer significant advantages, including enhanced security, stateful connections, support for access control lists (ACLs), and integrated support for Kerberos authentication. NFSv4 also reduces network chatter by consolidating multiple operations into fewer RPC calls, improving performance, especially over high-latency links. Choosing NFSv4.1 or newer further enables the use of parallel NFS (pNFS), which distributes file access across multiple storage devices, improving scalability and performance in demanding workloads.

Proper network architecture is essential when deploying NFS. Because NFS relies on TCP/IP for client-server communication, ensuring that both client and server systems are connected through a high-speed, low-latency network is crucial. In production environments, particularly where many clients access the same NFS exports, a dedicated storage network or VLAN can help isolate NFS traffic from general business applications and reduce network congestion. Using link aggregation techniques such as LACP (Link Aggregation Control Protocol) or deploying 10GbE or faster interfaces provides additional bandwidth and redundancy for NFS traffic, minimizing bottlenecks and improving resiliency.

Server hardware configuration must also be optimized for NFS workloads. A performant NFS server requires ample CPU power, especially when handling encryption or complex ACL processing. Memory is critical for effective caching, and deploying sufficient RAM allows for file system data and metadata to be retained in memory, reducing disk I/O and improving client response times. Disk subsystems should be designed based on workload characteristics. For example, high-throughput workloads benefit from SSDs or NVMe drives, while archival or backup data may be more suitable for traditional spinning disks in RAID configurations. Ensuring that the underlying file system is optimized for NFS workloads is also important. File systems like XFS or ext4 are common choices, and tuning parameters such as block size or journaling options should be adjusted according to expected usage patterns.

Export configurations on the NFS server must be meticulously defined to balance security and usability. The /etc/exports file specifies which directories are shared and the options applied to each export. It is recommended to limit exports to specific IP addresses or subnets to reduce unauthorized access risks. Export options such as read-only (ro), root_squash, and no_root_squash must be carefully considered. Root squashing is a common best practice in production environments as it prevents root users on client machines from having root-level access to NFS-mounted file systems, mitigating the risk of privilege escalation attacks. In contrast, environments requiring root access for specific automation tasks should weigh the security implications before disabling this option.

Authentication and encryption practices are another vital component of a secure NFS deployment. While NFSv3 and earlier versions rely on IP-based security, NFSv4 supports Kerberos authentication via RPCSEC_GSS, enabling secure, ticket-based user authentication. Configuring Kerberos in conjunction with NFS ensures that only authenticated users can access exported file systems, aligning with enterprise security policies. In environments where NFS traffic traverses untrusted networks, additional encryption measures such as VPN tunnels or IPsec should be implemented to protect data in transit, as NFS alone does not provide full end-to-end encryption of payloads.

Client configuration is equally important when deploying NFS. Consistency across clients can be achieved by standardizing mount options in /etc/fstab or automating the process using configuration management tools like Ansible or Puppet. Recommended mount options include specifying the NFS version explicitly, setting appropriate read (rsize) and write (wsize) buffer sizes to optimize throughput, and enabling hard mounts with timeouts and retransmission settings to improve resiliency in the event of server unavailability. Implementing automounters such as autofs can help reduce the risk of stale mounts and ensure NFS shares are mounted only when needed, conserving client-side resources.

Monitoring and logging are essential for the long-term success of an NFS deployment. Administrators should implement comprehensive monitoring for both the NFS server and clients. Tools like nfsstat, iostat, or system performance monitoring suites such as Nagios, Zabbix, or Prometheus can provide valuable insights into network utilization, RPC statistics, disk I/O, and resource usage. These metrics allow administrators to proactively identify performance bottlenecks and potential failure points. Log files generated by NFS daemons and system log services should be centralized and retained according to organizational policies. Forwarding logs to SIEM platforms supports audit requirements and enhances visibility into access patterns and potential security incidents.

High availability and redundancy planning are key best practices for business-critical NFS services. Implementing NFS in a clustered configuration with tools like Pacemaker and Corosync provides failover capabilities, ensuring that services remain available in the event of server failure. Additionally, combining NFS with shared storage backends, such as Storage Area Networks (SANs) or distributed file systems, allows multiple NFS servers to access the same storage pool, further enhancing redundancy and load balancing. In high-performance environments, deploying pNFS enables clients to parallelize file access across multiple storage nodes, reducing latency and improving throughput.

Data protection strategies such as backups and disaster recovery planning must not be overlooked. NFS shares should be included in regular backup routines, leveraging tools like rsync, snapshot technologies, or enterprise backup solutions that integrate with NFS. Replicating critical NFS exports to remote sites or cloud platforms provides an additional layer of protection against data loss and enables rapid recovery in the event of catastrophic failures.

Documentation and change management processes are also crucial. All NFS configurations, including export definitions, client mount settings, and network architecture diagrams, should be documented thoroughly. Maintaining version control for configuration files and adopting formal change management practices ensure that any modifications to the NFS infrastructure are traceable and can be rolled back if necessary.

By following these best practices, organizations can deploy NFS with confidence, ensuring that the system is secure, scalable, and capable of supporting demanding workloads. Whether used for shared application data, user home directories, or large-scale research environments, NFS remains a core technology in modern IT infrastructures when deployed and maintained according to proven strategies.

Optimizing NFS for Cloud-Native Workloads

As organizations transition to cloud-native architectures, optimizing Network File System (NFS) for these dynamic and distributed environments becomes increasingly critical. NFS, a protocol traditionally associated with on-premises file sharing, has adapted to meet the demands of modern workloads deployed on cloud platforms and container orchestration systems such as Kubernetes. Cloud-native workloads are characterized by their scalability, elasticity, and microservices-driven designs, which require storage solutions that can seamlessly integrate with ephemeral compute instances and dynamically shifting resource demands. To fully leverage NFS in cloud-native environments, it is essential to focus on tuning performance, enhancing flexibility, and ensuring resilient storage architectures that align with cloud principles.

One of the most significant factors in optimizing NFS for cloud-native workloads is the deployment model itself. In cloud settings, NFS is often implemented as a fully managed service provided by cloud vendors, such as Amazon Elastic File System (EFS), Azure NetApp Files, or Google Cloud Filestore. These services offer built-in scalability, automated patching, and elastic throughput, allowing developers and operations teams to provision NFS-compatible storage without the overhead of managing the underlying infrastructure. However, optimizing NFS in these environments still requires careful consideration of factors such as network latency, mount options, and client configurations to ensure peak performance and reliability.

Performance tuning for NFS in cloud-native workloads typically begins with selecting the appropriate NFS version. Modern workloads should leverage NFSv4.1 or higher, which provides improvements such as compound procedures to reduce round trips, integrated file locking, and support for Parallel NFS (pNFS). NFSv4.1 enhances performance in

177

distributed systems by enabling clients to perform parallel I/O operations across multiple storage nodes, helping alleviate bottlenecks associated with single-server architectures. For cloud-native applications deployed in Kubernetes clusters or autoscaling groups, this translates to more predictable and scalable file access as the number of compute nodes fluctuates.

Network performance is another key aspect of optimization. Since NFS operates over TCP/IP, minimizing network latency and ensuring sufficient bandwidth are critical for high-performance file access. In cloud environments, administrators should deploy NFS services within the same virtual private cloud (VPC) or region as the consuming workloads to reduce latency. Using cloud-native features such as enhanced networking (e.g., Amazon's Elastic Network Adapter or Azure Accelerated Networking) can further improve NFS performance by lowering network overhead and reducing jitter. For Kubernetes deployments, creating dedicated network policies or service meshes that prioritize NFS traffic can help guarantee consistent throughput and minimize contention with other workloads.

At the client level, tuning mount options is essential to optimizing NFS performance for cloud-native workloads. Adjusting the read (rsize) and write (wsize) buffer sizes to the maximum supported values for both clients and servers can reduce the number of I/O operations required for large file transfers, improving throughput. Enabling hard mounts with appropriate timeout and retransmission settings enhances resilience by allowing clients to recover from transient network interruptions without crashing. Additionally, using the noatime mount option can improve performance by preventing unnecessary metadata updates when files are read, which is particularly useful in read-heavy workloads typical of content delivery or machine learning pipelines.

In containerized environments, such as Kubernetes, optimizing NFS integration involves leveraging Persistent Volumes (PVs) backed by NFS. Administrators can provision dynamic or static PVs linked to NFS exports and use Persistent Volume Claims (PVCs) to abstract storage requests from application pods. Automating NFS PV provisioning using storage classes or Container Storage Interface (CSI) drivers ensures that cloud-native workloads can scale elastically without manual intervention. Additionally, configuring Kubernetes pod affinity rules and node selectors allows administrators to schedule workloads closer to NFS storage endpoints, reducing network latency and improving application responsiveness.

To ensure availability and resilience, NFS optimization must include redundancy and fault-tolerance strategies. In cloud-native deployments, NFS-backed storage should be distributed across multiple availability zones or regions to protect against localized outages. Managed NFS services offered by cloud providers often include high-availability features by default, replicating data across multiple physical storage nodes. For self-managed NFS solutions, administrators should implement clustered NFS servers or use distributed file systems that expose NFS gateways, such as CephFS or GlusterFS, to provide automatic failover and data redundancy.

Security optimization is a growing priority as cloud-native workloads often span public and private networks. NFS should be configured to enforce access controls through NFSv4 ACLs or by integrating with cloud-native identity and access management (IAM) solutions. Additionally, encrypting NFS traffic in transit using VPNs or enabling NFS over TLS, where supported, protects sensitive data from interception. For workloads subject to regulatory compliance, such as HIPAA or GDPR, auditing NFS access logs and integrating them into centralized SIEM platforms ensures that storage activity is monitored, and incidents can be quickly identified and addressed.

Automation is integral to optimizing NFS for cloud-native workloads. Infrastructure-as-Code (IaC) tools such as Terraform or AWS CloudFormation can be used to automate the provisioning and configuration of NFS services, ensuring consistency across environments and reducing human error. Similarly, configuration management tools like Ansible or Helm charts for Kubernetes can automate the deployment of NFS clients, mount configurations, and application workloads. Automation enables teams to rapidly scale NFS-backed storage in response to fluctuating demands, supporting the elasticity required in modern cloud-native environments.

Cost optimization is another dimension of NFS tuning in the cloud. Many managed NFS services offer multiple performance tiers or pricing models based on throughput, storage capacity, or access patterns. By analyzing workload characteristics and usage metrics, administrators can select the most appropriate storage tier to balance cost and performance. For instance, frequently accessed datasets may reside on premium storage tiers with high IOPS, while archival data can be moved to lower-cost storage classes with reduced performance requirements. Using lifecycle policies to automate data tiering ensures that storage costs remain under control without sacrificing performance for active workloads.

Monitoring and observability complete the optimization cycle for NFS in cloud-native workloads. Leveraging cloud-native monitoring tools such as Amazon CloudWatch, Azure Monitor, or open-source solutions like Prometheus and Grafana, administrators can track key performance indicators including I/O throughput, latency, and error rates. By setting up proactive alerts and visualizing performance trends, teams can quickly identify bottlenecks, predict capacity requirements, and continuously refine configurations to meet evolving workload demands.

Optimizing NFS for cloud-native workloads requires a holistic approach that encompasses infrastructure design, client configurations, automation, and continuous performance monitoring. As cloud-native paradigms emphasize agility, scalability, and resilience, fine-tuning NFS implementations to meet these objectives ensures that applications benefit from efficient and reliable file access. Whether supporting containerized microservices, distributed data pipelines, or hybrid cloud architectures, NFS remains a valuable component in enabling organizations to build robust and scalable storage solutions in the era of cloud-native computing.

Final Thoughts and Recommendations

Network File System (NFS) has established itself as one of the most versatile and enduring technologies for network-based file sharing. Its longevity is a testament to its simplicity, flexibility, and ability to adapt to evolving technological landscapes. From small business networks to large-scale enterprise environments, NFS has remained a critical component in the delivery of shared storage services. Despite the rise of alternative storage solutions, including distributed file systems, object storage, and cloud-native offerings, NFS continues to play an integral role in supporting a variety of workloads across on-premises and cloud infrastructures.

One of the key strengths of NFS lies in its ability to operate across heterogeneous environments. Whether deployed on Unix, Linux, macOS, or even Windows systems through third-party implementations, NFS facilitates seamless data sharing among different operating systems. This interoperability is essential in organizations with diverse IT infrastructures that must support legacy applications, modern cloud workloads, and everything in between. The ability of NFS to provide a common file-sharing protocol simplifies the task of connecting disparate systems and reduces the need for complex file transfer workflows.

The evolution of NFS has kept it relevant in a rapidly changing IT world. The introduction of NFSv4 brought significant improvements, including stateful protocol design, integrated security features through Kerberos authentication, and the ability to apply Access Control Lists (ACLs) for fine-grained permission management. These enhancements have made NFS suitable for secure and enterprise-grade deployments, addressing concerns that earlier versions, such as NFSv3, lacked native security mechanisms. Organizations deploying NFS today should adopt at least NFSv4.1 to benefit from these advanced features and avoid the limitations and risks associated with older protocol versions.

In addition to protocol improvements, best practices in NFS deployment have evolved. Modern recommendations include segregating NFS traffic onto dedicated storage networks, using high-speed network interfaces, and configuring server and client settings to optimize performance and reliability. The importance of proper export configurations cannot be overstated, as misconfigurations may lead to unauthorized access or introduce vulnerabilities. Enforcing root squashing, defining strict client IP access rules, and deploying Kerberos-based authentication are all considered essential security measures.

Administrators should also recognize that NFS, while reliable, is not inherently designed for every workload. In high-performance computing (HPC) environments or big data scenarios where large datasets are accessed concurrently by hundreds of clients, distributed file systems such as Lustre, CephFS, or GlusterFS may offer performance and scalability benefits that exceed what traditional NFS can provide. However, for workloads such as home directories, application configuration storage, and shared document repositories, NFS remains an efficient and well-supported solution.

The integration of NFS with modern cloud services further underscores its continued relevance. Cloud providers such as AWS, Azure, and Google Cloud offer managed NFS-compatible services that combine the ease of use and elasticity of the cloud with the familiarity of NFS. By adopting these services, organizations can extend existing NFS workflows into hybrid or multi-cloud environments without major rearchitecting. This flexibility makes NFS a valuable bridge between legacy systems and modern cloud-native applications, facilitating gradual cloud adoption strategies without disrupting business operations.

Automation plays a significant role in modern NFS management. By incorporating Infrastructure-as-Code (IaC) tools and configuration management solutions such as Terraform, Ansible, or Puppet, organizations can automate the provisioning, configuration, and scaling of NFS servers and clients. Automation ensures consistency, reduces human error, and accelerates deployment times, especially in environments where agility and rapid scalability are key priorities. Automated monitoring and alerting solutions, often integrated with SIEM platforms or DevOps toolchains, further enhance the operational reliability of NFS deployments by enabling proactive issue detection and resolution.

Security remains a critical area of focus for NFS deployments. In addition to enforcing strong authentication and access control measures, organizations must implement encryption for NFS traffic traversing public or shared networks. While NFS itself does not natively encrypt data payloads, network-level encryption via VPN tunnels or IPsec ensures that sensitive information is protected during transmission. Administrators should also ensure that NFS log data is centralized, retained according to compliance requirements, and regularly reviewed for signs of unauthorized access or anomalous behavior.

Looking ahead, the role of NFS in cloud-native architectures and containerized environments is likely to grow. Kubernetes and other container orchestration platforms increasingly support NFS as a storage backend, enabling persistent storage for stateful applications and microservices. The use of Persistent Volumes (PVs) and dynamic provisioning allows for seamless integration of NFS with containerized workloads, enhancing storage flexibility and supporting elastic scaling of applications. As NFS evolves, deeper integration with cloud-native tools and storage orchestration frameworks will position it as a key player in modern DevOps workflows.

While performance tuning is often workload-specific, general recommendations include optimizing server and client buffer sizes, adjusting the number of nfsd threads on servers, and monitoring both disk I/O and network throughput to ensure that NFS environments remain responsive under load. Enterprises with latency-sensitive applications or large-scale user bases should consider leveraging NFSv4.1's support for parallel NFS (pNFS), which enhances performance by allowing clients to access multiple data servers concurrently.

Disaster recovery and high availability are additional priorities that should be incorporated into any NFS deployment strategy. Implementing clustered NFS servers with automatic failover capabilities ensures that critical storage services remain available even in the face of hardware failures or site outages. Pairing NFS with robust backup solutions and data replication strategies helps protect against data loss, enabling organizations to quickly recover from both localized and widespread disruptions.

Ultimately, NFS remains a proven and adaptable solution for networked file storage. Its continued development and integration into modern infrastructures ensure that it will remain a valuable tool for organizations managing shared data across diverse environments. By adhering to best practices in security, performance tuning, and automation, IT teams can maximize the value of NFS while supporting both legacy systems and cutting-edge cloud-native applications.

The future of NFS lies not in replacing new technologies, but in complementing them. As hybrid and multi-cloud environments become the norm and containerization redefines how applications are deployed, NFS will continue to evolve to meet the needs of both traditional and modern workloads. Organizations that invest in optimizing and securing their NFS deployments will benefit from a versatile and reliable storage platform that is well-suited to the demands of today's dynamic IT landscape.